The Millennium Starts at Field House.!

This book has been
placed in the
Leslie Price
Memorial Library
by

June Blay

Friend of Christine & Alex Hawkes

EASTERN ASIA AND CLASSICAL GREECE

THE ILLUSTRATED
HISTORY OF THE WORLD

VOLUME 2

EASTERN ASIA AND CLASSICAL GREECE

J. M. ROBERTS

DUNCAN BAIRD PUBLISHERS

LONDON

The Illustrated History of the World

This edition first published in Great Britain in 1999

Duncan Baird Publishers
Sixth Floor
Castle House
75–76 Wells Street
London W1P 3RE

EASTERN ASIA AND CLASSICAL GREECE
Copyright © Editorial Debate SA 1998
Text Copyright © J. M. Roberts 1976, 1980, 1983, 1987, 1988, 1992, 1998
Artwork and Diagrams Copyright © Editorial Debate SA 1998
(for copyright of photographs and maps, see acknowledgments on page 192, which are to
be regarded as an extension of this copyright)

Art Direction by Duncan Baird Publishers.
Produced by Duncan Baird Publishers, London, England,
and Editorial Debate, Madrid, Spain.

British Library Cataloguing-in-Publication Data.
A catalogue record for this book is available from the British Library.

ISBN 1-900131-77-3

DBP team:
Senior editor: Joanne Levêque
Assistant editor: Georgina Harris
Senior designer: Steven Painter
Assistant designer: Anita Schnable
Picture research: Julia Ruxton
Sales fulfilment: Ian Smalley
Map artwork: Russell Bell
Commissioned artwork: Gillie Newman, Stephen Conlin
Decorative borders: Lorraine Harrison

Editorial Debate team:
Editors and picture researchers:
Isabel Belmonte Martínez, Feliciano Novoa Portela,
Ruth Betegón Díez, Dolores Redondo
Editorial coordination: Ana Lucía Vila

Typeset in Sabon 11/15 pt
Colour reproduction by Trescan, Madrid, Spain
Printed in Singapore by Imago Limited

NOTE
The abbreviations CE and BCE are used throughout this book:
CE Common Era (the equivalent of AD)
BCE Before Common Era (the equivalent of BC)

10 9 8 7 6 5 4 3 2 1

CONTENTS

THE BEGINNINGS OF CIVILIZATION IN EASTERN ASIA

As contacts between them multiplied, the isolation of the oldest civilizations in the Near East was steadily broken down. From that interplay emerged a more cosmopolitan, if still highly differentiated, world of cultural traditions. Yet at the same time areas of the world in which other civilizations had appeared (only a little later, in the timescales of early history) remained almost untouched by what happened in the area delimited by the Aegean, Egypt and Iran. There is no need to look further than distance and topography for explanations. Yet the consequences of remoteness and inaccessibility were very important. What took place in northern China and the Indian sub-continent was to shape cultural traditions in remote places for thousands of years. As centres for the diffusion of civilized life they long remained impervious to outside cultural influence; little more than peripheral and occasional contact with other zones of civilization was possible until a very long time had gone by. The outcome was the establishment of cultural traditions over large areas which contained elements which would be strong enough to endure even through periods of intimate connexion with other traditions; even in this century, the institution of caste long dominated Indian thinking about society, and Confucian ideas once enshrined in the curriculum for the imperial examinations system still shaped the ideas of the Chinese literati. The influence of China and India was also to spread far beyond their own physical limits or later political frontiers and the spheres of influence they created are still visible today. The influence of these traditions was widespread and powerful. From the standpoint of world history they were of vast importance.

During the 3rd century BCE, the first Buddhist *stupas* (commemorative burial mounds) were constructed in India. The Great Stupa in Sanchi (right) was built in around 220 BCE, almost three centuries after the Buddha's death. Its domed shape symbolizes both the master's tomb and the cosmic egg, which represents the original universe in Indian scriptures. The enormous carved gateway was erected in the 1st century CE.

1 ANCIENT INDIA

EVEN NOW, ANCIENT INDIA is still visible and accessible to us in a very direct sense. At the beginning of this century, some Indian communities still lived as all our primeval ancestors must once have lived, by hunting and gathering. The bullock-cart and the potter's wheel of many villages today are, as far as can be seen, identical with those used four thousand years ago. A caste system whose main lines were set by about 1000 BCE still regulates the lives of millions, and even of some Indian Christians and Moslems. Gods and goddesses whose cults can be traced to the Stone Age are still worshipped at village shrines.

INDIAN DIVERSITY

In some ways ancient India is with us still as is no other ancient civilization. Yet although such examples of the conservatism of Indian

The Indus valley

The first Indian civilization emerged more than 4,000 years ago in the valley carved by the great Indus River, which is fed by snow and glacial meltwater from its source in the Himalayas. On the Punjab Plains, the Indus is further swollen by tributaries such as the Sutlej and the Jhelum, bringing water from the mighty Punjab River to the east.

The remains of many ancient settlements have been discovered in the Indus valley region, including those of the cities of Mohenjo-Daro in the south and Harappa in the north.

Map showing the cities of the early Indus valley civilization.

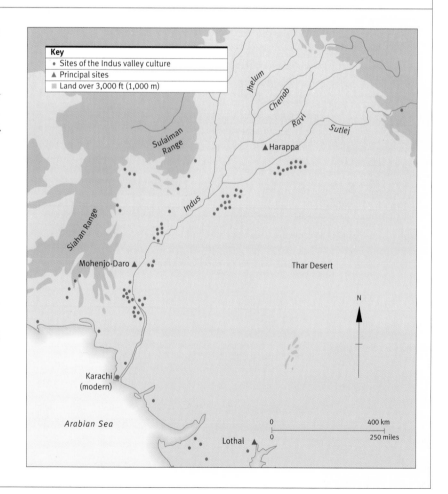

Key
- Sites of the Indus valley culture
- ▲ Principal sites
- ■ Land over 3,000 ft (1,000 m)

The Khyber Pass is the most famous of the routes through the mountains along India's northwestern border, linking the highlands of Afghanistan and the fertile Indus valley. The route has frequently been used to invade India.

life are commonplace, the country that contains them contains many other things too. The hunter-gatherers of the early twentieth century were the contemporaries of other Indians used to travelling in railway trains. The diversity of Indian life is enormous, but wholly comprehensible given the size and variety of its setting. The sub-continent is, after all, about the size of Europe and is divided into regions that are clearly distinguished by climate, terrain and crops. There

are two great river valleys, the Indus and Ganges systems, in the north; between them lie desert and arid plains, and to the south the highlands of the Deccan, largely forested. When written history begins, India's racial complexity, too, is already very great: scholars identify six main ethnic groups. Many others were to arrive later and make themselves at home in the Indian sub-continent and society, too. All this makes it hard to find a focus.

This small limestone bust found at Mohenjo-Daro is one of the most famous archaeological pieces from the first Indian civilization, that of the Indus valley. Thought to represent a priest or a king, the bearded figure has a band tied around his forehead. His dress – a tunic covering one shoulder – is similar to that of contemporary Mesopotamian figures of kings.

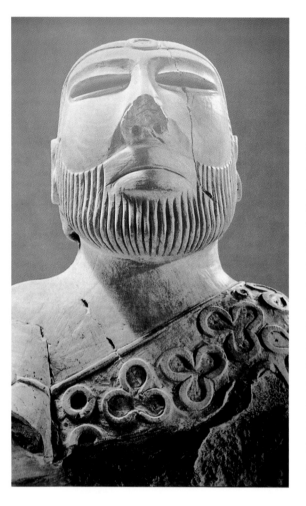

outside world by geography. In spite of her size and variety, until the oceans began to be opened up in the sixteenth and seventeenth centuries CE, India had only to grapple with occasional, though often irresistible, incursions by alien peoples. To the north and northwest she was protected by some of the highest mountains in the world; to the east lay belts of jungle. The other two sides of the sub-continent's great triangle opened out into the huge expanses of the Indian ocean. This natural definition not only channelled and restricted communication with the outside world; it also gave India a distinctive climate. Much of India does not lie in the tropics, but none the less that climate is tropical. The mountains keep away the icy winds of Central Asia; the long coasts open themselves to the rain-laden clouds which roll in from the oceans and cannot go beyond the northern ranges. The climatic clock is the annual monsoon, bringing the rain during the hottest months of the year. It is still the central prop of an agricultural economy.

GEOGRAPHICAL INSULATION

Indian history has a unity in the fact of its enormous power to absorb and transform forces playing on it from the outside. This provides a thread to guide us through the patchy and uncertain illumination of its early stages which is provided by archaeology and texts long transmitted only by word of mouth. Its basis is to be found in another fact, India's large measure of insulation from the

INFLUENCES FROM THE NORTH

Protected in some measure from external forces though she has always been before modern times, India's north-western frontier is more open than her others to the outside world. Baluchistan and the frontier passes were the most important zones of encounter between India and other peoples right down to the seventeenth century CE; in civilized

Time chart (2250 BCE–185 BCE)				
2250–1750 BCE Zenith of the Harappan civilization			700–500 BCE Upanishads composed	321–185 BCE Maurya Dynasty: first Indian empire
2000 BCE	1500 BCE	1000 BCE	500 BCE	
1750 BCE Aryan invasion begins	1500–1000 BCE Vedic hymns composed		563–483 BCE Life of the Buddha	

times even India's contacts with China were first made by this roundabout route (though it is not quite as roundabout as Mercator's familiar projection makes it appear). At times, this northwestern region has fallen directly under foreign sway, which is suggestive when we consider the first Indian civilizations; we do not know much about the way in which they arose but we know that Sumer and Egypt antedated them. Mesopotamian records of Sargon I of Akkad report contacts with a "Meluhha" which scholars have believed to be the Indus valley, the alluvial plains forming the first natural region encountered by travellers once they have entered India. It was there, in rich, heavily forested countryside, that the first Indian civilizations appeared at the time when, farther west, the great movements of Indo-European peoples were beginning to act as the levers of history. There may have been more than one stimulus at work.

The evidence also shows that agriculture came later to India than to the Near East. It, too, can first be traced in the sub-continent in its northwest corner. There is archaeological evidence of domesticated animals in Baluchistan as far back as 3700 BCE. By 3000 BCE there are signs of settled life on the alluvial plains and parallels with other river-valley cultures begin to appear. Wheel-thrown pottery and copper implements begin to be found. All the signs are of a gradual build-up in intensity of agricultural settlements until true civilization appears as it did in Egypt and Sumer. But there is the possibility of direct Mesopotamian influence in the background and, finally, there is at least a reasonable inference that already India's future was being shaped by the coming of new peoples from the north. At a very early date the complex racial composition of India's population suggests this, though it would be rash to be assertive about it.

When at last indisputable evidence of civilized life is available, the change is startling.

Archaeological excavations have revealed the advanced town planning that characterized the cities of the Harappan culture built more than 4,000 years ago. The Mohenjo-Daro citadel's Great Bath, pictured here, had a fountain and a drainage system. The pool was rendered watertight by a thick layer of bitumen.

One scholar speaks of a cultural "explosion". There may have been one crucial technological step, the invention of burnt brick (as opposed to the sun-baked mud brick of Mesopotamia) which made flood control possible in a flat plain lacking natural stone. Whatever the process, the outcome was a remarkable civilization which stretched over a half-million square miles of the Indus valley, an area greater than either the Sumerian or Egyptian.

THE HARAPPAN CIVILIZATION

THIS CIVILIZATION HAS BEEN GIVEN the name "Harappan", because one of its great sites is the city of Harappa on a tributary of the Indus. There is another such site at Mohenjo-Daro; others are being discovered. Together they reveal human beings highly organized and capable of carefully regulated collective works on a scale equalling those of Egypt and Mesopotamia. There were large granaries in the cities, and weights and measures seem to have been standardized over a large area. It is a clear that a well-developed culture was established by 2250 BCE and lasted for something like four hundred years with very little change.

The two cities which are its greatest monuments may have contained more than thirty thousand people each. This says much for the agriculture which sustained them; the region was then far from being the arid zone it later became. Mohenjo-Daro and Harappa were between two and two and a half miles in circumference and the uniformity and complexity of their building speaks for a very high degree of administrative and organizational skill. They each had a citadel and a residential area; streets of houses were laid out on rectangular grid plans and made

A mong the objects discovered during excavations at the ancient city of Harappa, in the north of present-day Pakistan, was this stone gaming board.

of bricks of standardized sizes. Both the elaborate and effective drainage systems and the internal layout of the houses show a strong concern for bathing and cleanliness; in some streets of Harappa nearly every house has a bathroom. Perhaps it is not fanciful to see in this some of the first manifestations of what has become an enduring feature of Indian religion, the bathing and ritual ablutions which are still important to Hindus.

HARAPPAN CULTURE

Before 2000 BCE, the inhabitants of Mohenjo-Daro and Harappa were trading far afield and living an economic life of some complexity. A great dockyard, connected by a mile-long canal to the sea at Lothal, four hundred miles south of Mohenjo-Daro, suggests the importance of an external trade which reached, through the Persian Gulf, as far north as Mesopotamia. In the Harappan cities themselves evidence survives of specialized craftsmen drawing their materials from a wide area and subsequently sending out again across its length and breadth the products of their skills. This civilization had cotton cloth

This figurine from the Harappa culture, found at Mohenjo-Daro, represents a slender, naked young woman, adorned with a necklace and numerous bracelets. It is thought that the girl was probably a dancer.

Thousands of small, square Harappan seals have been found. Mainly made of soapstone, most of the stamps depict animal figures, including unicorns, bulls, buffaloes and tigers. Most of the stamps are inscribed; although some 2,000 different inscriptions have been discovered, they have yet to be deciphered.

(the first of which we have evidence) which was plentiful enough to wrap bales of goods for export whose cordage was sealed with seals found at Lothal. These seals are part of our evidence for Harappan literacy; a few inscriptions on fragments of pottery are all that supplements them and provides the first traces of Indian writing. The seals, of which about 2,500 survive, provide some of our best clues to Harappan ideas. The pictographs on the seals run from right to left. Animals often appear on them and may represent six seasons into which the year was divided. Many "words" on the seals remain unreadable, but it now seems at least likely that they are part of a language akin to the Dravidian tongues still used in southern India.

THE DIFFUSION OF HARAPPAN CIVILIZATION

Ideas and techniques from the Indus spread throughout Sind and the Punjab, and down the west coast of Gujarat. The process took centuries and the picture revealed by archaeology is too confused for a consistent pattern to emerge. Where its influence did not reach – the Ganges valley, the other great silt-rich area where large populations could live, and the southeast – different cultural processes were at work, but they have left nothing so spectacular behind them. Some of India's culture must derive from other sources; there are traces elsewhere of Chinese influence. But it is hard to be positive. Rice, for example, began to be grown in India in the Ganges valley; we simply do not know where it came from, but one possibility is China or South-East Asia, on whose coasts it was grown from about 3000 BCE. Two thousand years later, this crucial item in Indian diet was used over most of the north.

THE END OF HARAPPAN CIVILIZATION

We do not know why the first Indian civilizations began to decline, although their passing can be roughly dated. The devastating floods of the Indus or uncontrollable alterations of its course may have wrecked the delicate balance of the agriculture on its banks. The forests may have been destroyed by tree-felling to provide fuel for the brick-kilns on which Harappan building depended. But perhaps there were also other agencies at work. Skeletons, possibly those of men killed where they fell, were found in the streets of Mohenjo-Daro. Harappan civilization seems to end in the Indus valley about 1750 BCE and this coincides strikingly with the irruption into Indian history of one of its great creative forces, the invading Aryans, though scholars do not favour the idea that invaders destroyed the Indian valley cities. Perhaps the newcomers entered a land already devastated by over-exploitation and natural disasters.

ARYAN INVASION

Strictly speaking, "Aryan" is a linguistic term, like "Indo-European". None the less, it has customarily and conveniently been used to identify one group of those Indo-European peoples whose movements make up so much of the dynamic of ancient history in other parts of the Old World after 2000 BCE. At about the time when other Indo-Europeans were flowing into Iran, somewhere about 1750 BCE, a great influx of Aryans began to

enter India from the Hindu Kush. This was the beginning of centuries during which waves of these migrants washed deeper and deeper into the Indus valley and the Punjab and eventually reached the upper Ganges. They did not obliterate the native peoples, though the Indus valley civilization crumbled. No doubt much violence marked their coming, for the Aryans were warriors and nomads, armed with bronze weapons, bringing horses and chariots, but they settled and there are plenty of signs that the native populations lived on with them, keeping their own beliefs and practices alive. There is much archaeological evidence of the fusion of Harappan with later ways. However qualified, this was an early example of the assimilation of cultures which was always to characterize Indian society and was eventually to underly classical Hinduism's remarkable digestive power.

ARYAN CULTURE

IT SEEMS CLEAR that the Aryans brought to India no culture so advanced as that of the Harappans. It is a little like the story of the coming of Indo-Europeans in the Aegean. Writing, for example, disappears and does not emerge again until the middle of the first millennium BCE; cities, too, have to be re-invented and when they are again to be found they lack the elaboration and order of their Indus valley predecessors. Instead, the Aryans appear to have slowly given up their pastoral habits and settled into agricultural life, spreading east and south from their original settlement areas in a sprawl of villages. This

A clay figurine from Mohenjo-Daro. Scholars think this woman, who is wearing a short skirt, a belt, abundant long necklaces and a tall headdress, may have been a dancer.

A number of Harappan clay figurines depicting a cart being pulled by two oxen have been found. The imprints of ancient wheels have also been discovered, and evidence suggests that the Harappan carts were very similar to the ones still used in the region today.

took centuries. Not until the coming of iron was it complete and the Ganges valley colonized; iron implements made cultivation easier. Meanwhile, together with this physical opening up of the northern plains, Aryan culture had made two decisive contributions to Indian history, in its religious and in its social institutions.

ARYAN RELIGION

The Aryans laid the foundations of the religion which has been the heart of Indian civilization. Theirs centred on sacrificial concepts; through sacrifice the process of creation which the gods achieved at the beginning of time was to be endlessly repeated. Agni, the god of fire, was very important, because it was through his sacrificial flames that people could reach the gods. Great importance and standing was given to the *brahmans*, the priests who presided over these ceremonies. There was a pantheon of gods of whom two of the most important were Varuna, god of the heavens, controller of natural order and the embodiment of justice, and Indra, the warrior god who, year after year, slew a dragon and thus released again the heavenly waters which came with the breaking of the monsoon. We learn about them from the *Rig-Veda*, a collection of more than a thousand hymns performed during sacrifice, collected for the first time in about 1000 BCE but certainly accumulated over centuries. It is one of our most important sources for the history not only of Indian religion but also of Aryan society.

THE *RIG-VEDA*

The *Rig-Veda* seems to reflect an Aryan culture as it has been shaped by settlement in India and not Aryan culture as it had existed at earlier times. It is, like Homer, the eventual written form of a body of oral tradition, but quite different in being much less difficult to use as a historical source, since its status is much more certain. Its sanctity made its memorization in exact form essential, and though the *Rig-Veda* was not to be written down until after 1300 CE, it was then still almost certainly largely uncorrupted from its original form. Together with later Vedic

Harappan streets followed very regular grid-plan layouts, as can be seen in this street in Mohenjo-Daro's lower city. Most of the houses in this part of the town had bathrooms and remarkably advanced drainage and sanitary systems.

Agni, the Vedic god of fire, is depicted on this bas-relief. He is surrounded by a halo of flames and his mount, a goat, appears at his feet. Agni was the most commonly invoked Vedic god – a beneficial figure who brought light and warmth. His flames were also believed to purify sacrifices, making them acceptable to other divinities.

hymns and prose works, it is our best source for Aryan India, whose archaeology is cramped for a long time because building materials less durable than the brick of the Indus valley cities were used in its towns and temples.

There is a suggestion again of the world of Homer in the world revealed by the *Rig-Veda*, which is one of Bronze Age barbarians. Some archaeologists now believe they can identify in the hymns references to the destruction of the Harappan cities. Iron is not mentioned and appears only to have come to India after 1000 BCE (there is argument about how late and from what source). The setting of the hymns is a land which stretches from the western banks of the Indus to the Ganges, inhabited by Aryan peoples and dark-skinned native inhabitants. These formed societies whose fundamental units were families and tribes, but the legacies of these were less enduring than the pattern of Aryan social organization which eventually emerges and which we call caste.

THE CASTE SYSTEM

About the early history of the vast and complicated subject of the caste system and its implications it is impossible to speak with assurance. Once the rules of caste were written down, they appeared as a hard and solid structure, incapable of variation. Yet this did not happen until caste had been in existence for hundreds of years, during which it was still flexible and evolving. Its root appears to be a recognition of the fundamental class-divisions of a settled agricultural society, a warrior-aristocracy (*kshatriyas*), priestly

brahmans and the ordinary peasant-farmers (*vaishyas*). These are the earliest divisions of Aryan society which can be observed and seem not to have been exclusive; movement between them was possible. The only unleapable barrier in early times seems to have been that between non-Aryans and Aryans; one of the words used to denote the aboriginal inhabitants of India by Aryans was *dasa*, which came eventually to denote "slave". To the occupational categories was soon added a fourth category for non-Aryans. Clearly it rested on a wish to preserve racial integrity. These were the *shudras*, or "unclean", who might not study or hear the Vedic hymns.

This structure has been elaborated almost ever since. Further divisions and subdivisions appeared as society became more complex and movements within the original threefold structure took place. In this the *brahmans*, the highest class, played a crucial role.

This 13th-century CE bas-relief portrays Varuna, the Vedic god of justice. He carries a coil of rope for tying up criminals.

Landowners and merchants came to be distinguished from farmers; the first were called *vaishyas*, and *shudras* became cultivators. Marriage and eating taboos were codified. This process gradually led to the appearance of the caste system as we know it. A vast number of castes and sub-castes slowly inserted themselves into the system. Their obligations and demands eventually became a primary regulator of Indian society, perhaps the only significant one in many Indians' lives. By modern times there were thousands of *jatis* – local castes with members restricted to marrying within them, eating only food cooked by fellow-members, and obeying their regulations. Usually, too, a caste limited those who belonged to it to the practice of one craft or profession. For this reason (as well as because of the traditional ties of tribe, family and locality and the distribution of wealth) the structure of power in Indian society right down to the present day has had much more to it than formal political institutions and central authority.

POLITICAL SYSTEMS

In early times Aryan tribal society threw up kings, who emerged, no doubt, because of military skill. Gradually, some of them acquired something like divine sanction, though this must always have depended on a nice balance of relations with the *brahman* caste. But this was not the only political pattern. Not all Aryans accepted this evolution. By about 600 BCE, when some of the detail of early Indian political history at last begins to be dimly discernible through a mass of legend and myth, two sorts of political communities can be discerned, one non-monarchical, tending to survive in the hilly north, and one monarchical, established in the Ganges valley. This reflected centuries of

On this bas-relief Indra, the Vedic warrior god, rides an elephant and brandishes his favourite weapon, the thunderbolt, or *vajra*. Indra was believed to be an invincible fighter and the Aryans invoked his protection in battle.

steady pressure by the Aryans towards the east and south during which peaceful settlement and intermarriage seem to have played as big a part as conquest. Gradually, during this era, the centre of gravity of Aryan India had shifted from the Punjab to the Ganges valley as Aryan culture was adopted by the peoples already there.

THE GANGES VALLEY

As we emerge from the twilight zone of the Vedic kingdoms, it is clear that they established something like a cultural unity in northern India. The Ganges valley was by the seventh century BCE the great centre of Indian population. It may be that the cultivation of rice made this possible. A second age of Indian cities began there, the first of them market-places and centres of manufacture, to judge by the way they brought together specialized craftsmen. The great plains, together with the development of armies on a larger and better-equipped scale (we hear of the use of elephants), favoured the consolidation of larger political units. At the end of the seventh century BCE, northern India was organized in sixteen kingdoms, though how this happened and how they were related to one another is still hard to disentangle from their mythology. None the less, the existence of coinage and the beginnings of writing make it likely that they had governments of growing solidity and regularity.

The processes in which they emerged are touched on in some of the earliest literary sources for Indian history, the *Brahmanas*, texts composed during the period when Aryan culture came to dominate the Ganges valley (c.800–600 BCE). But more about them and the great names involved can be found in later documents, above all in two great Indian epics, the *Ramayana* and the *Mahabharata*. The present texts are the result of constant revision from about 400 BCE to 400 CE, when they were written down as we know them for the first time, so their interpretation is not easy. In consequence, it remains hard to get at the political and administrative reality behind, say, the kingdom of Magadha, based on southern Bihar, which emerged eventually as the preponderant power and was to be the core of the first historical empires of India. On the other hand (and possibly more importantly), the evidence is clear that the Ganges valley was already what it was to remain, the seat of empire, its cultural domination assured as the centre of Indian civilization, the future Hindustan.

THE NORTH–SOUTH DIVIDE

The later Vedic texts and the general richness of the Aryan literary record make it all too easy to forget the existence of half the subcontinent. Written evidence tends to confine Indian history down to this point (and even after) to the history of the north. The state of archaeological and historical scholarship also reflects and further explains the concentration of attention on northern India. There is just much more known about it in ancient times than about the south. But there are also better and less accidental justifications for such an emphasis. The archaeological evidence shows, for example, a clear and continuing cultural lag in this early period between the area of the Indus system and the rest of India (to which, it may be remarked, the river was to give its name). Enlightenment (if it may be so expressed) came from the north. In the south, near modern Mysore,

This small terracotta plaque, dating from the 2nd century BCE, was found in Kaushambi and is a fine example of early Indian sculpture. The sumptuous throne upon which the two lovers are seated suggests that the work may represent a prince and his bride, perhaps on their wedding night.

This 3rd-century BCE capital originally crowned a polished stone pillar inscribed with the precepts of the Maurya emperor of India, Asoka (264–228 BCE). The four lions, standing back-to-back on the wheel of law, are now the symbol of the modern-day Indian Union.

settlements roughly contemporaneous with Harappa show no trace of metal, though there is evidence of domesticated cattle and goats. Bronze and copper only begin to appear at some time after the Aryan arrival in the north. Once outside the Indus system, too, there are no contemporary metal sculptures, no seals and fewer terracotta figures. In Kashmir and eastern Bengal there are strong evidences of Stone Age cultures with affinities with those of south China, but it is at least clear that, whatever the local characteristics of the Indian cultures with which they were in contact and within the limits imposed by geography, first Harappan and then Aryan civilization was dominant. They gradually asserted themselves towards Bengal and the Ganges valley, down the west coast towards Gujarat, and in the central highlands of the sub-continent. This is the pattern of the Dark Age, and when we reach that of history, there is not much additional light. The survival of Dravidian languages in the south shows the region's persistent isolation.

TOPOGRAPHICAL DIFFERENTIATION

Topography explains much of this isolation. The Deccan has always been cut off from the north by jungle-clad mountains, the Vindhya. Internally, too, the south is broken and hilly, and this did not favour the building of large states as did the open plains of the north. Instead, south India remained fragmented, some of its peoples persisting, thanks to their inaccessibility, in the hunting and gathering cultures of a tribal age. Others, by a different accident of geography, turned to the

Indian epic literature

The two oldest known epic texts of Hindu literature are the *Mahabharata* and the *Ramayana*. Although originally written in about 400 BCE, they relate events that took place in India between the years 1400 and 1000 BCE. The first text consists of various legendary subjects that surround a central theme: the fight for power between two families, the Kauravas and the Pandavas. But, most importantly, the *Mahabharata* is an exposition of *dharma*, a moral code governing how a warrior, a king, or anyone who wants to be included in the cycle of rebirth, should act. One of the most beautiful passages, the *Bhagavad Gita* (*The Song of the Lord*), constitutes (along with the Upanishads) the basic religious scriptures for Hinduism. The second poem, the *Ramayana*, narrates the life of Rama, the incarnation of Vishnu, who is hailed as the perfect king and man.

Hanuman, the flying monkey-god, features in the Ramayana *as one of Rama's loyal generals.*

A scene from the *Ramayana* is depicted in this 18th-century manuscript illustration: Rama, the poem's protagonist, and his younger brother Laksmana are wandering in search of Rama's wife, Sita. In the poem, Rama shows himself to be a virtuous warrior, completely loyal to the aristocratic code of honour.

seas – another contrast with the predominantly agrarian empires of the north.

INDIAN RELIGIONS

MILLIONS OF PEOPLE must have been affected by the changes so far described. Estimates of ancient populations are notoriously unreliable. India's has been put at about 25 millions in 400 BCE, which would be roughly a quarter of the whole population of the world at that time. The importance of India's early history nevertheless lies in the way it laid down patterns still shaping the lives of even larger numbers today, rather than in its impact on big populations in antiquity. This is above all true of religion. Classical Hinduism crystallized in the first millennium BCE. A great world religion, Buddhism, was also launched then in India; it eventually dominated wide areas of

Asia. What people do is shaped by what they believe they can do; it is the making of a culture that is the pulse of Indian history, not the making of a nation or an economy, and to this culture religion was central.

SHIVA

The deepest roots of the Indian religious and philosophical synthesis go very deep indeed. One of the great popular cult figures of the Hindu pantheon today is Shiva, in whose worship many early fertility cults have been brought together. A seal from Mohenjo-Daro already shows a figure who looks like an early Shiva, and stones like the *lingam* found in modern temples, the phallic cult-object which is his emblem, have been found in the Harappan cities. There is some presumptive evidence therefore for the view that worship of Shiva may be the oldest surviving religious

The central element of the *Mahabharata* is the struggle of the five Pandavas brothers against their cousins, the hundred Kauravas princes. In this scene, the Kauravas armies are attacking the army of Abhimanyu, the son of Arjuna.

Mysticism and mythology in ancient India

Vedic and *Brahman* literature, which is the oldest source of knowledge of Hindu mythology and mysticism, encompasses a range of works, from the *Rig-Veda* to the Upanishads.

The great historian of Indian philosophy, Surendranath Dasgupta, distinguishes four different types of mysticism. The first type is gathered in Vedic and *Brahman* literature (the *Vedas*, 1500–1000 BCE) and focuses on the control of nature and the gods through ritual. The second type of mysticism, gathered in the texts called Upanishads (1000–500 BCE), contains a number of philosophical speculations about the nature of the universe and the position of man within it. The third, the *yoga*, is related to control of the body and the mind. The fourth, the Buddhist, dates from the 6th century BCE and uses control of the body and the mind for the realization of the four Truths (the existence of pain, the causes of pain, the cessation of pain and how to arrive at these truths) and the achievement of *nirvana* (freedom from all desires). These types of mysticism have several common

elements: all are based on experience and can be communicated, all aim to free the spirit from matter, all state that in order to achieve this, control over the body and mind are vital. They also all state that knowledge does not consist of analysis, but of directly approaching one's inner self.

This 12th-century CE bas-relief depicts, from left to right, the three main gods of the classical Hindu pantheon: Brahma, first being to be created and creator of all things; Vishnu, a social and good god, preserver of the world; and Shiva, the contradictory god of destruction, asceticism and procreation.

cult in the world. Though he has assimilated many important Aryan characteristics, he is pre-Aryan and survives in all his multi-faceted power, still an object of veneration today. Nor is Shiva the only possible survival from the remote past of Indus civilization. Other Harappan seals seem to suggest a religious world centred about a mother-goddess and a bull. The bull survives to this day, the Nandi of countless village shrines all over Hindu India (and newly vigorous in his latest incarnation, as the electoral symbol of the Congress Party).

VISHNU

Vishnu, another focus of modern popular Hindu devotion, is much more an Aryan.

Vishnu joined hundreds of local gods and goddesses still worshipped today to form the Hindu pantheon. Yet his cult is far from being either the only or the best evidence of the Aryan contribution to Hinduism. Whatever survived from the Harappan (or even pre-Harappan) past, the major philosophical and speculative traditions of Hinduism stem from Vedic religion. These are the Aryan legacy. To this day, Sanskrit is the language of religious learning; it transcends ethnic divisions, being used in the Dravidian-speaking south as much as in the north by the *brahman*. It was a great cultural adhesive and so was the religion it carried. The Vedic hymns provided the nucleus for a system of religious thought more abstract and philosophical than primitive animism. Out of Aryan notions of hell and paradise, the House of Clay and the

World of the Fathers, there gradually evolved the belief that action in life determined human destiny. An immense, all-embracing structure of thought slowly emerged, a world view in which all things are linked in a huge web of being. Souls might pass through different forms in this immense whole; they might move up or down the scale of being, between castes, for example, or even between the human and animal worlds. The idea of transmigration from life to life, its forms determined by proper behaviour, was linked to the idea of purgation and renewal, to the trust in liberation from the transitory, accidental and apparent,

Brahma, creator of the universe, was a focus of early worship. His prestige began to decline as Vishnu and Shiva became more popular. Here he appears riding a wild goose, whose flight symbolizes the soul's efforts to free itself.

and to belief in the eventual indentity of soul and absolute being in *Brahma*, the creative principle. The duty of the believer was the observation of *Dharma* – a virtually untranslatable concept, but one which embodies something of the western ideas of a natural law of justice and something of the idea that people owed respect and obedience to the duties of their station.

THE *BRAHMANS*

These developments took a long time. The steps by which the original Vedic tradition began its transformation into classical Hinduism are obscure and complicated. At the centre of the early evolution had been the *brahmans* who long controlled religious thought because of their key role in the sacrificial rites of Vedic religion. The brahmanical class appears to have used its religious authority to emphasize its seclusion and privilege. To kill a *brahman* soon became the gravest of crimes; even kings could not contend with their powers. Yet they seem to have come to terms with the gods of an older world in early times; it has been suggested that it may have been the infiltration of the brahmanical class by priests of the non-Aryan cults which ensured the survival and later popularity of the cult of Shiva.

S hiva is a complex and contradictory god, destroyer and restorer, ascetic and sensual. He represents the Hindu idea of combining complementary qualities in one personality. In this bronze statue from the Chola kingdom (9th to 12th centuries CE), he is depicted as the lord of dance.

THE UPANISHADS

The sacred Upanishads, texts dating from about 700 BCE, mark the next important evolution towards a more philosophical religion.

They are a mixed bag of about two hundred and fifty devotional utterances, hymns, aphorisms and reflexions of holy men pointing to the inner meaning of the traditional religious truths. They give much less emphasis to personal gods and goddesses than earlier texts and also include some of the earliest ascetic teachings which were to be so visible and striking a feature of Indian religion, even if only practised by a small minority. The Upanishads met the need felt by some to look outside the traditional structure for religious satisfaction. Doubt appears to have been felt about the sacrificial principle. New patterns of thought had begun to appear at the beginning of the historical period and uncertainty about traditional beliefs is already expressed in the later hymns of the *Rig-Veda*. It is convenient to mention such developments here because they cannot be understood apart from the Aryan and pre-Aryan past. Classical Hinduism was to embody a synthesis of ideas like those in the Upanishads (pointing to a monistic conception of the universe) with the more polytheistic popular tradition represented by the *brahmans*.

JAINISM

Abstract speculation and asceticism were often favoured by the existence of monasticism, a stepping-aside from material concerns to practise devotion and contemplation. The practice appeared in Vedic times. Some monks threw themselves into ascetic experiment, others pressed speculation very far and we have records of intellectual systems which rested on outright determinism and materialism. One very successful cult which did not require belief in gods and expressed a reaction against the formalism of the brahmanical religion was Jainism, a creation of a sixth-century teacher who, among other things, preached a respect for animal life which made agriculture or animal husbandry impossible. Jains therefore tended to become merchants, with the result that in modern times the Jain community is one of the wealthiest in India.

This detail from a 19th-century CE painting portrays Vishnu riding his mount Garuda, the magical eagle. Garuda, whose mission was to defend humanity against demons, was also revered as a god.

The Chandogya Upanishad

"That hidden essence you do not see, dear one,
From that a whole nyagrodha tree will grow.
There is nothing that does not come from him.
Of everything he is the inmost Self.
He is the truth; he is the Self supreme.
You are that, Shvetaketu; you are that."
"Please, Father, tell me more about this Self."
"Yes, dear one, I will," Uddalaka said.
"Place this salt in water and bring it here
Tomorrow morning." The boy did.
"Where is that salt?" his father asked.
"I do not see it."
"Sip here. How does it taste?"
"Salty, Father."
"And here? And there?"
"I taste salt everywhere."
"It *is* everywhere, though we see it not.
Just so, dear one, the Self is everywhere,
Within all things, although we see him not.
There is nothing that does not come from him.
Of everything he is the inmost Self.
He is the truth; he is the Self supreme.
You are that, Shvetaketu; you are that."

An extract from the Chandogya Upanishad, translated by Eknath Easwaran.

THE BUDDHA

The first images of the Buddha were carved at the beginning of the Common Era. Some of the most impressive of these sculptures are situated in the caves at Ajanta, in central India. From the 2nd century BCE to the 7th century CE, communities of Buddhist monks inhabited the caves, using them as temples.

By far the most important of the innovating systems was the teaching of the Buddha, the "enlightened one" or "aware one" as his name may be translated.

It has been thought significant that the Buddha, like some other religious innovators, was born in one of the states to the northern edge of the Ganges plain where the orthodox, monarchical pattern emerging elsewhere did not establish itself. This was early in the sixth century BCE. Siddhartha Gautama was not a *brahman*, but a prince of the warrior class.

The *Dammapadha*

"Vigilance is the realm of immortality; negligence is the realm of death. People who are vigilant do not die; people who are negligent are as if dead.
The wise, with thorough knowledge of vigilance, enjoy being vigilant and delight in the realm of the noble.
Meditative, persevering, always striving diligently, the wise attain *nirvana*, supreme peace.
Energetic, alert, pure in deed, careful in action, self-controlled, living in accord with truth the vigilant one will rise in repute.
By energy, vigilance, self-control, and self-mastery, the wise one may make an island that a flood cannot sweep away.
Fools, unintelligent people, indulge in heedlessness. The wise one, however, guards vigilance as the best of riches.
Do not indulge in negligence, do not be intimate with attachment to desire. The vigilant one, meditating, gains great happiness.
When the sage expels negligence by vigilance, climbing the tower of insight, the wise one, sorrowless, gazes upon the sorrowing, ignorant crowd below, as one on a mountain peak views people on the ground.
Vigilant among the heedless, awake among the sleeping, the wise one goes ahead like a racehorse outstripping a nag.
Indra became highest of the deified by vigilance. Vigilance they praise; negligence is always censured.
The mendicant who delights in vigilance, fearing negligence, goes along like a fire burning up bondage, subtle and gross.
The mendicant who delights in vigilance, fearing negligence, cannot fall away, being near to *nirvana* already".

An extract from "Vigilance" from the *Dammapadha*, translated by Thomas Cleary.

After a comfortable and gentlemanly up-
bringing he found his life unsatisfying and
left home. His first recourse was asceticism.
Seven years of this proved to him that he
was on the wrong road. He began instead
to preach and teach. His reflexions led him to
propound an austere and ethical doctrine,
whose aim was liberation from suffering by
achieving higher states of consciousness. This
was not without parallels in the teaching of
the Upanishads.

BUDDHIST PHILOSOPHY

An important part in Buddhism was to be
played by *yoga*, which was to become one
of what were termed the "Six Systems" of
Hindu philosophy. The word has many mean-
ings but in this context is roughly translatable
as "method" or "technique". It sought to
achieve truth through meditation after a complete and perfect control of the body had been
attained. Such control was supposed to reveal
the illusion of personality which, like all else

in the created world, is mere flux, the passage
of events, not identity. This system, too, had
already been sketched in the Upanishads and
was to become one of the aspects of Indian
religion which struck visitors from Europe
most forcibly. The Buddha taught his disciples so to discipline and shed the demands of
the flesh that no obstacle should prevent the
soul from attaining the blessed state of
nirvana or self-annihilation, freedom from
the endless cycle of rebirth and transmigration, a doctrine urging people not to do
something, but to be something – in order not
to be anything. The way to achieve this was
to follow an Eightfold path of moral and spir-
itual improvement. All this amounts to a
great ethical and humanitarian revolution.

THE LEGACY OF THE BUDDHA

The Buddha apparently had great practical
and organizing ability which, together with
his unquestionable personal quality, quickly
made him a popular and successful teacher.

Monastic communities transformed these natural caves, at Ajanta in the Maharashtra state in western India, into one of the country's most impor-tant and most richly decorated monuments. After its heyday in the 5th and 6th centuries CE, the site was aban-doned and was not rediscovered until the early 19th century CE.

Although there are no early Indian images of the Buddha as a man, several representations of his footprints exist. This pair, surrounded by a lotus-petal motif symbolizing purity and wisdom, is from Bodh Gaya, where the enlightenment of the Buddha took place.

He sidestepped, rather than opposed, the brahmanical religion and this must have smoothed his path. The appearance of communities of Buddhist monks gave his work an institutional setting which would outlive him. He also offered a role to those not satisfied by traditional practice, in particular to women and to low-caste followers, for caste was irrelevant in his eyes. Finally, Buddhism was non-ritualistic, simple and atheistic. It soon underwent elaboration, and, some would say, speculative contamination, and like all great religions it assimilated much preexisting belief and practice, but by doing so it retained great popularity.

Yet Buddhism did not supplant brahmanical religion and for two centuries or so was confined to a relatively small part of the Ganges valley. In the end, too – though not until well into the Common Era – Hinduism was to be the victor and Buddhism would dwindle to a minority belief in India. But it was to become the most widespread religion in Asia and a potent force in world history. It is the first world religion to spread beyond the society in which it was born, for the older tradition of Israel had to wait for the Common Era before it could assume a world role. In its native India, Buddhism was to be important until the coming of Islam. The teaching of the

This figure, which adorned the doorway of the Great Stupa at Sanchi, depicts a *yakshi*, one of the benign deities who made trees blossom and were incorporated into the Buddhist creed. The *yakshi*'s headdress and jewellery are similar to those of figurines found at Mohenjo-Daro, suggesting the continuation of a cultural heritage begun 2,000 years previously.

Buddha marks, therefore, a recognizable epoch in Indian history; it justifies a break in its exposition. By his day, an Indian civilization still living today and still capable of enormous assimilative feats stood complete in its essentials. This was a huge fact; it would separate India from the rest of the world.

CONTINUITY OF EARLY INDIAN CIVILIZATION

Much of the achievement of early civilization in India remains intangible. There is a famous figure of a beautiful dancing-girl from Mohenjo-Daro, but ancient India before the Buddha's time did not produce great art on the scale of Mesopotamia, Egypt, or Minoan Crete, far less their great monuments. Marginal in her technology, she came late – though how much later than other civilizations cannot be exactly said – to literacy, too. Yet the uncertainties of much of India's early history cannot obscure the fact that her social system and her religions have lasted longer than any other great creations of the mind. Even to guess at what influence they exercised through the attitudes they encouraged, diffused through centuries in pure or impure forms, is rash. Only a negative dogmatism is safe; so comprehending a set of world views, institutions so careless of the individual, philosophy so assertive of the relentless cycles of being, so lacking in any easy ascription of responsibility for good and evil, cannot but have made a history very different from that of human beings reared in the great Semitic traditions. And these attitudes were formed and settled for the most part a thousand years before Christ.

2 ANCIENT CHINA

Although the original Great Wall was built at the end of the 3rd century BCE, the wall sections that are still standing mainly date back to the Ming Dynasty (14th to 17th century CE).

THE MOST STRIKING FACT of China's history is that it has gone on for so long. For about two and a half thousand years there has been a Chinese nation using a Chinese language. Its government as a single unit has long been taken to be normal, in spite of intervals of division and confusion. China has had a continuing experience of civilization rivalled in duration only by that of ancient Egypt. This experience is the key to Chinese historical identity; it is as much cultural as political. The example of India shows how much more important culture can be than government, and China's makes the same point in a different way; in China, culture made unified government easier. Somehow at a very early date she crystallized certain institutions and attitudes which were to endure because they suited her circumstances. Some of them seem even to transcend the revolution of the twentieth century.

TOPOGRAPHY

We must begin with the land itself, and at first sight it does not suggest much that makes for unity. The physical theatre of Chinese history is vast. China is bigger than the United States and now contains three to four times as many people. The Great Wall which guarded the northern frontier was made up of between 2,500 and 3,000 miles of fortifications and has never been completely surveyed. From Peking to Hong Kong, more or less due south, is 1,200 miles as the crow flies. This huge expanse contains many climates and many regions. One great distinction stands out among them, that between northern and southern China. In summer the north is scorching and arid while the south is humid and used to floods; the north looks bare and dustblown in the winter, while the south is always green. This is not all that this distinction implies. One of the major themes of early Chinese history is of the spread of civilization, sometimes by migration, sometimes by diffusion, from north to south, of the tendency of conquest and political unification to take the same broad direction, and of the continual stimulation and irrigation of northern civilization by currents from the outside, from Mongolia and Central Asia.

China's major internal divisions are set by mountains and rivers. There are three great river valleys which drain the interior and run across the country roughly from west to east. They are, from north to south, the Hwang-Ho,

Physical map of China

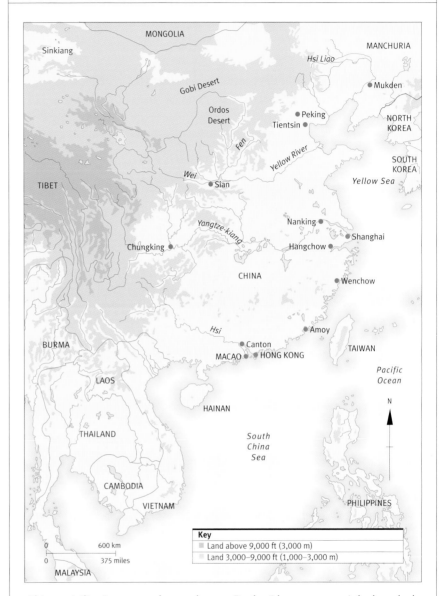

Chinese civilization emerged more than 3,000 years ago in the Yellow River valley, cold in winter but with fertile loess lands. From this area, civilization began to extend gradually southwards. By the 6th century BCE, it had reached the Yangtze valley and under the Han Dynasty (202 BCE–220 CE) the Chinese world also included the tropical lands that reach the sea in southern China.

Time chart (1700 BCE–221 BCE)

c.1700–1050 BCE Shang period	722–481 BCE Period of the Springs and Autumns	221 BCE Unification of China by Shih-Huang-ti, First Emperor
900 BCE	600 BCE	300 BCE
1050–771 BCE Western Chou period	403–221 BCE Period of the Warring States	

or Yellow River, the Yangtze and the Hsi. It is surprising that a country so vast and thus divided should form a unity at all. Yet China is isolated, too. One scholar thinks the country a world by itself since the start of the Pliocene. Much of China is mountainous and except in the extreme south and northeast her frontiers still sprawl across and along great ranges and plateaux. The headwaters of the Yangtze, like those of the Mekong, lie in the high Kunlun, north of Tibet. These highland frontiers are great insulators. The arc they form is broken only where the Yellow River flows south into China from inner Mongolia and it is on the banks of this river that the story of civilization in China begins.

THE ROLE OF THE YELLOW RIVER

Skirting the Ordos desert, itself separated by another mountain range from the desolate wastes of the Gobi, the Yellow River opens a sort of funnel into north China. Through it have flowed people and soil; the loess beds of the river valley, easily worked and fertile, laid down by wind from the north, are the basis of the first Chinese agriculture. Once this region was richly forested and well watered, but it became colder and more desiccated in one of those climatic transformations which are behind so much primeval social change. To Chinese pre-history overall, of course, there is a bigger setting than one river valley. "Peking man" turns up as a fire-user about six hundred thousand years ago, and there are Neanderthal traces in all three of the great river basins. The trail from these forerunners to the dimly discernible cultures which are their successors in early Neolithic times, leads us to a China already divided into two cultural zones, with a meeting place and mixing area on the Yellow River. It is impossible to separate the tangle of cultural

This curve lies in the stretch of the great Yellow River that crosses the Ordos desert, to the north of the fertile lands where Chinese civilization first emerged.

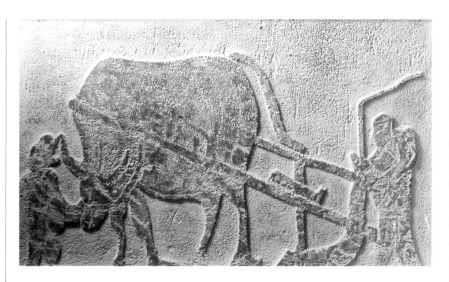

An image of a man using an ox-drawn plough was found on this brick from a Han-period tomb in China's Szechwan province.

interconnexions already detectable by that time. But there was no even progress towards a uniform or united culture; even in early historical times, we are told, "the whole of China ... was teeming with Neolithic survivals". Against this varied background emerged settled agriculture; nomads and settlers were to coexist in China until our own day. Rhinoceros and elephant were still hunted in the north not long before 1000 BCE.

THE IMPACT OF AGRICULTURE

As in other parts of the world, the coming of agriculture meant a revolution. It has been argued that peoples who lived in the semi-tropical coastal areas of South-East Asia and south China were clearing forests to make fields as far back as 10,000 BCE. Certainly they exploited vegetation to provide themselves with fibres and food. But this is still a topic about which much more needs to be known. A much better record exists in northern China where ground just above the flood level of the Yellow River begins to yield evidence of agriculture from about 5000 BCE. Somewhat like that of early Egypt, it seems to have been exhaustive or semi-exhaustive. The land was cleared, used for a few years, and then left to revert to nature while the cultivators turned attention elsewhere. From this area agriculture can be seen later to spread both north to Manchuria and to the south. It has been called the "nuclear area of North China". Within it there soon appeared complex cultures which combined with agriculture the use of jade and wood for carving, the domestication of silkworms, the making of ceremonial vessels in forms which were to become traditional and perhaps even the use of chopsticks. In other words, this was in Neolithic times already the home of much that is characteristic of the Chinese tradition of historic times.

A pottery vase from the Neolithic culture of Longshan, which flourished in southern China in the 3rd millennium BCE. The strange shapes of many of these vases, painstakingly made with very thin sides, suggest that they were designed for ritual rather than everyday use.

This highly decorative cooking vessel is made of bronze and dates from Chinese Shang Ding period (c.16th–11th centuries BCE).

EARLY SOCIETY

Ancient writers recognized the importance of this revolutionary social change and legends identified a specific inventor of agriculture, yet very little can be inferred confidently or clearly about social organization at this stage. Perhaps because of this there has been a persistent tendency among Chinese to idealize it.

Long after private property had become widespread it was assumed that "under heaven every spot is the sovereign's ground" and this may reflect early ideas that all land belonged to the community as a whole. The Chinese Marxists have maintained this tradition, discerning in the archaeological evidence a golden age of primitive Communism preceding a descent into slave and feudal society.

Argument is unlikely to convince those interested in the question one way or the other. Ground seems to be firmer in attributing to these times the appearance of a clan structure and totems, with prohibitions on marriage within the clan. Kinship in this form is almost the first institution which can be seen to have survived to be important in historical times. The evidence of the pottery, too, suggests some new complexity in social roles. Already things were being made which cannot have been intended for the rough and tumble of everyday use; a stratified society seems to be emerging before we reach the historical era.

One material sign of a future China already obvious at this stage is the widespread use of millet, a grain well adapted to the sometimes arid farming of the north. It was to be the basic staple of Chinese diet until about a thousand years ago and sustained a society which in due course arrived

at literacy, at a great art of bronze-casting based on a difficult and advanced technology, at the means of making exquisite pottery far finer than anything made anywhere else in the world, and, above all, at an ordered political and social system which identifies the first major age of Chinese history. But it must be remembered once more that the agriculture which made this possible was for a long time confined to north China and that many parts of this huge country only took up farming when historical times had already begun.

THE SHANG DYNASTY

The narrative of early times is very hard to recover, but can be outlined with some confidence. It has been agreed that the story of civilization in China begins under rulers from a people called the Shang, the first name with independent evidence to support it in the traditional list of dynasties which was for a long time the basis of Chinese chronology. From the late eighth century BCE we have better dates, but we still have no chronology for early Chinese history as well founded as, say, that of Egypt. It is more certain that somewhere about 1700 BCE (and a century each way is an acceptable margin of approximation) a tribe called the Shang, which enjoyed the military advantage of the chariot, imposed itself on its neighbours over a sizable stretch of the Yellow River valley. Eventually, the Shang domain was a matter of about 40,000 square miles in northern Honan; this made it somewhat smaller than modern England, though its cultural influences reached far beyond its periphery, as evidence from as far away as south China, Chinese Turkestan and the northeastern coast shows.

Shang kings lived and died in some state; slaves and human sacrificial victims were

Bronze ritual axes, such as this one from the Shang period, were used to decapitate victims during sacred ceremonies. Human sacrifice was common in Shang-period China. Often hundreds of people were sacrificed during the burial ceremonies that accompanied the funerals of kings.

Yet Shang government was advanced enough to use scribes and had a standardized currency. What it could do when at full stretch is shown in its ability to mobilize large amounts of labour for the building of fortifications and cities.

THE CHOU DYNASTY

Shang China succumbed in the end to another tribe from the west of the valley, the Chou. A probable date is 1027 BCE. Under the Chou, many of the already elaborate governmental and social structures inherited from the Shang were preserved and further refined. Burial rites, bronze-working techniques and decorative art also survived in hardly altered forms. The great work of the Chou period was the consolidation and diffusion of this heritage. In it can be discerned the hardening of the institutions of a future Imperial China which would last two thousand years.

The Chou thought of themselves as surrounded by barbarian peoples waiting for the benevolent effects of Chou tranquillization (an idea, it may be remarked, which still underlay the persistent refusal of Chinese officials two thousand years later to regard diplomatic missions from Europe as anything but respectful bearers of tribute). Chou supremacy in fact rested on war, but from it flowed great cultural consequences. As under the Shang, there was no truly unitary state and Chou government represented a change of degree rather than kind. It was usually a matter of a group of notables and vassals, some more dependent on the dynasty than others, offering in good times at least a formal acknowledgement of its supremacy and all increasingly sharing in a common culture. Political China (if it is reasonable to use such a term) rested upon big estates which had

Jade was a much prized material in ancient China. This ritual dagger dates from the beginning of the Shang period in the 2nd millennium BCE and has a jade blade.

This bronze lid from a ritual vase dates from the period of the Western Chou and depicts a stylized animal head.

buried with them in deep and lavish tombs. Their courts had archivists and scribes, for this was the first truly literate culture east of Mesopotamia. This is one reason for distinguishing between Shang civilization and Shang dynastic paramountcy; this people showed a cultural influence which certainly extended far beyond any area they could have dominated politically. The political arrangements of the Shang domains themselves seem to have depended on the uniting of landholding with obligations to a king; the warrior landlords who were the key figures were the leading members of aristocratic lineages with semi-mythical origins.

This 17th-century CE watercolour is entitled "Don't gamble with danger" and illustrates the story of King You of the Chou Dynasty, who lost the empire because he wanted to make the queen laugh.

sufficient cohesion to have powers of long survival and in this process their original lords turned into rulers who could be called kings, served by elementary bureaucracies.

THE PERIOD OF WARRING STATES

The Chou system collapsed from about 700 BCE, when a barbarian incursion drove the Chou from their ancestral centre to a new home farther east, in Honan. The dynasty did not end until 256 BCE, but the next distinguishable epoch dates from 403 to 221 BCE and is significantly known as the Period of the Warring States. In it, historical selection by conflict grew fierce. Big fish ate little fish until one only was left and all the Chinese lands were for the first time ruled by one great empire, the Ch'in, from which the country

Tang "the Victorious", founder of the Shang Dynasty, is shown walking in the country-side in this 17th-century CE watercolour. According to legend, Tang came across people catching birds and persuaded them to let the birds go free, a gesture which won him great popularity.

was to get its name. This is matter for discussion elsewhere; here it is only apropos in that it registers an epoch in Chinese history.

Reading about these events in the traditional Chinese historical accounts can produce a slight feeling of beating the air, and historians who are not experts in Chinese studies may perhaps be forgiven if they cannot trace over this period of some fifteen hundred years or so any helpful narrative thread in the dimly discernible struggles of kings and over-mighty subjects. They should be; after all, scholars have not yet provided one. Nevertheless, two basic processes were going on for most of this time which were very important for the future and which give the period some unity, though their detail is elusive. The first of these was a continuing diffusion of culture outwards from the Yellow River basin.

To begin with, Chinese civilization was a matter of tiny islands in a sea of barbarism. Yet by 500 BCE it was the common possession of scores, perhaps hundreds, of "states" scattered across the north, and it had also been carried into the Yangtze valley. This had long been a swampy, heavily forested region very different from the north and inhabited by far more primitive peoples. Chou influence – in part thanks to military expansion – irradiated this area, and helped to produce the first major culture and state of the Yangtze valley, the Ch'u civilization. Although owing much to the Chou, it had many distinctive linguistic, calligraphic, artistic and religious traits of its own. By the end of the Period of Warring States we have reached the point at which the stage of Chinese history is about to be much enlarged.

These two jade figures date from the middle Western Chou period (10th century BCE). Because figures are rarely found in Shang or early Chou art, it is thought that these may have been imported or inspired by similar objects from southern or south-western China.

LANDOWNERS AND PEASANTS

The second of the fundamental and continuing processes that took place under both Shang and Chou was the establishment of landmarks in institutions which were to survive until modern times. Among them was a fundamental division of Chinese society into a landowning nobility and the common people. Most of these were peasants, making up the vast majority of the population and paying for all that China produced in the way of civilization and state power. What little we know of their countless lives can be quickly said; even less can be discovered than about the anonymous masses of toilers at the base of every other ancient civilization. There is one good physical reason for this: the life of the Chinese peasant was an alternation between his mud hovel in the winter and an encampment where he lived during the summer months to guard and tend his growing crops. Neither has left much trace. For the rest, he appears sunk in the anonymity of his community (he does not belong to a clan), tied to the soil, occasionally taken from it to carry out other duties and to serve his lord in war or hunting. His depressed state is expressed by the classification of modern Chinese communist historiography which lumps Shang and Chou together as "Slavery Society" preceding the "Feudal Society" which comes next.

THE NOBILITY

ALTHOUGH CHINESE SOCIETY was to grow much more complex by the end of the Warring States period, the distinction of common people from the nobly born remained. There were important practical consequences: the nobility, for example, were not subject to punishments – such as mutilation – inflicted on the commoner; it was a survival of this in later times that the gentry were exempt from the beatings which might be visited on the commoner (though, of course, they might suffer appropriate and even dire punishment for more serious crimes). The nobility long enjoyed a virtual monopoly of wealth, too, which outlasted its earlier monopoly of metal weapons. None the less, these were not the crucial distinctions of status, which lay elsewhere, in the nobleman's special religious standing through a monopoly of certain ritual practices. Only noblemen could share in the cults which were the heart of the Chinese notion of kinship. Only the nobleman belonged to a family – which meant that he had ancestors. Reverence for ancestors and propitiation of their spirits had existed before the Shang, though it does not seem that in early times many ancestors were thought likely to survive into the spirit world. Possibly the only ones lucky enough to do so would be the spirits of particularly important persons; the most likely, of course, were the rulers themselves, whose ultimate origin, it was claimed, was itself godly.

THE CLAN AND THE FAMILY

The family emerged as a legal refinement and subdivision of the clan, and the Chou period was the most important one in its clarification. There were about a hundred clans, within each of which marriage was forbidden. Each was supposed to be founded by a hero or a god. The patriarchal heads of the clan's families and houses exercised special authority over its members and were all qualified to carry out its rituals and thus influence spirits to act as intermediaries with the powers which controlled the universe on the clan's behalf. These practices came to identify persons entitled to possess land or hold office.

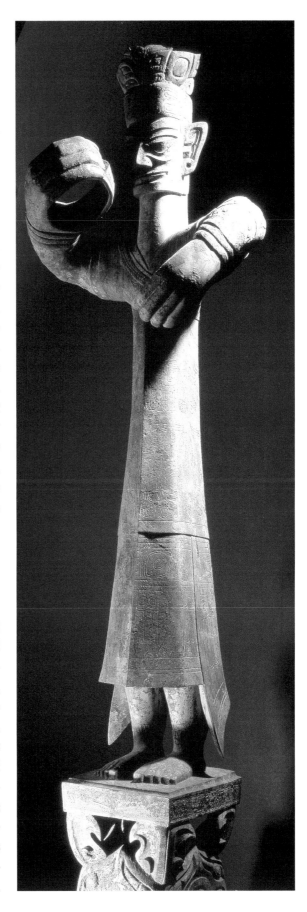

This bronze male figure on a base stands 8.5 ft (2.62 m) high and dates from the 12th century BCE (Shang period). Found in one of two sacrificial pits in the Szechwan province of China, the figure clearly once held an object – probably an elephant tusk – in his hands. His long robe is decorated with small figures.

The clan offered a sort of democracy of opportunity at this level: any of its members could be appointed to the highest place in it, for they were all qualified by the essential virtue of a descent whose origins were godlike. In this sense, a king was only *primus inter pares*, a patrician outstanding among all patricians.

RELIGION

THE FAMILY ABSORBED enormous quantities of religious feeling and psychic energy; its rituals were exacting and time-consuming. The common people, not sharing in this, found a religious outlet in maintaining the worship of nature gods. These always got some attention from the élite, too, the worship of mountains and rivers and the propitiating of their spirits being an important imperial duty from early times, but they were to influence the central developments of Chinese thought less than similar notions in other religions.

RELIGION AND POLITICAL FORMS

Religion had considerable repercussions on political forms. The heart of the ruling house's claim to obedience was its religious superiority. Through the maintenance of ritual, it had access to the goodwill of unseen powers, whose intentions might be known from the oracles. When these had been interpreted, the ordering of the agricultural life of the community was possible, for they regulated such matters as the time of sowing or harvesting. Much turned, therefore, on the religious standing of the king; it was of the first importance to the state. This was reflected in the fact that the Chou displacement of the Shang was religious as well as military. The idea was introduced that there existed a god superior to the ancestral god of the dynasty and that from him there was derived a mandate to rule. Now, it was claimed, he had decreed that the mandate should pass to other hands. This was the introduction of another idea fundamental to the Chinese conception of government and it

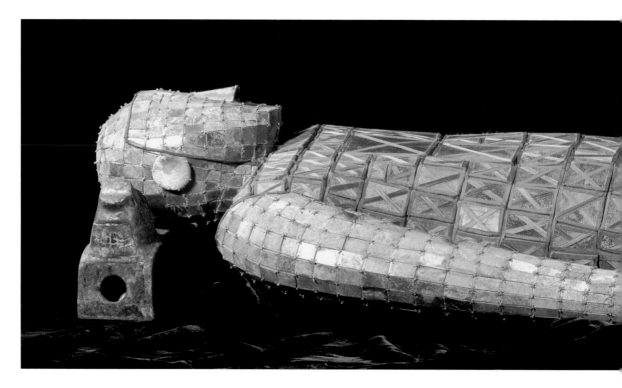

was to be closely linked to the notion of a cyclic history, marked by the repeated rise and fall of dynasties. Inevitably, it provoked speculation about what might be the signs by which the recipient of the new mandate should be recognized. Filial piety was one, and to this extent, a conservative principle was implicit. But the Chou writers also introduced an idea rendered not very comfortably into English by the word "virtue". Clearly, its content remained fluid; disagreement and discussion were therefore possible.

THE ROLE OF THE MONARCH

In its earliest forms the Chinese "state" – and over long periods one must think of more than one coexisting – seems little more than an abstraction from the idea of the ruler's estate and the necessity to maintain the rituals and sacrifices. The records do not leave an impression of a very busy monarchy. Apart from the extraordinary decisions of peace or war, the king seems to have had little to do except fulfil his religious duties, hunt, and initiate building projects in the palace complexes which appear as early as Shang times, though there are indications of Chou kings also undertaking (with the labour of prisoners) extensive agricultural colonization. For a long time the early Chinese rulers did without any very considerable bureaucracy. Gradually a hierarchy of ministers emerged who regulated court life, but the king was a landowner who for the most part needed only bailiffs, overseers and a few scribes. No doubt much of his life was spent on the move about his lands. The only other aspect of his activity which needed expert support was the supernatural. Out of this much was to grow, not least the intimate connexion between rule in China and the determination of time and the calendar, both very important in agricultural societies. These were based on astronomy, and though this came to have a respectable basis in observation and calculation, its origins were magical and religious.

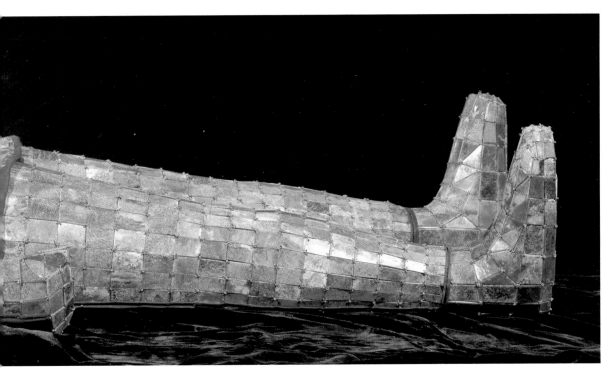

Prince Tou Wan's 2nd-century BCE burial suit, pictured here, is made of more than 2,000 small jade plates. The remains of 10 of these fantastic cocoons have been discovered – jade was believed to be a key to immortality. This practice reached the zenith of its popularity under the Han Dynasty. Expensive burials were later banned by an emperor who considered them to be a lure for grave robbers.

This bone oracle dates from the Shang period. The oldest Chinese inscriptions, of which several thousand exist, date from this period and have been found engraved on bone or on tortoise shells. The oracle was heated until it began to crack. The cracks were then interpreted to divine the spirits' answers to the questions posed.

THE USE OF ORACLES

In the earliest days all the great decisions of state, and many lesser ones, were taken by consulting oracles. This was done by engraving turtle shells or the shoulder-blades of certain animals with written characters and then applying to them a heated bronze pin so as to produce cracks on the reverse side. The direction and length of these cracks in relation to the characters would then be considered and the oracle read accordingly. This was an enormously important practice from the point of view of historians, for such oracles were kept, presumably as records. They also provide us with evidence for the foundation of Chinese language, for the characters on the oracle bones (and some early bronzes) are basically those of classical Chinese. The Shang had about 5000 such characters, though not all can be read. Nevertheless, the principles of this writing show a unique consistency; while other civilizations gave up pictographic characterization in favour of phonetic systems, the Chinese language grew and evolved, but remained essentially within the pictographic framework. Already under the Shang, moreover, the structure of the language was that of modern Chinese – monosyllabic and depending on word order, not on the inflection of words, to convey meaning. The Shang, in fact, already used a form of Chinese.

THE IMPORTANCE OF WRITING IN ANCIENT CHINA

Writing was to remain high on the scale of Chinese arts and has always retained some trace of the religious respect given to the first characters. Only a few years ago, examples of Mao Tse-tung's calligraphy were widely reproduced during his ascendancy and were used to enhance his prestige. This reflects the centuries during which writing remained the jealously guarded privilege of the élite. The readers of the oracles, the so-called *shih*, were the primitive form of the later scholar-gentry class; they were indispensable experts, the possessors of hieratic and arcane skills. Their monopoly was to pass to the much larger class of the scholar-gentry in later times. The language thus remained the form of communication of a relatively small élite which not only found its privileges rooted in its possession but also had an interest in preserving it against corruption or variation. It was of enormous importance as a unifying and stabilizing force because written Chinese became a language of government and culture transcending divisions of dialect, religion and region. Its use by the élite tied the country together.

THE FIRST IRON CASTING

Several great determinants of future Chinese history had thus been settled in outline by the end of the Chou period. That end came after increasing signs of social changes which were affecting the operation of the major institutions. This is not surprising; China long remained basically agricultural, and change was often initiated by the pressure of population upon resources. This accounts for the impact of the introduction of iron, probably in use by about 500 BCE. As elsewhere a sharp rise in agricultural production (and therefore in population) followed. The first tools which have been found come from the fifth century BCE; iron weapons came later. At an early date, too, tools were made by casting, for iron moulds for sickle blades have been found dating from the fourth or fifth centuries. Chinese technique in handling the new metal was thus advanced in very early

times. Whether by development from bronze casting or by experiments with pottery furnaces which could produce high temperatures, China somehow arrived at the casting of iron at about the same time as knowledge of how to forge it. Exact precedence is unimportant; what is noteworthy is that sufficiently high temperatures for casting were not available elsewhere for another nineteen centuries or so.

URBANIZATION

Another important change under the later Chou was a great growth of cities. They tended to be sited on plains near rivers, but the first of them had probably taken their shape and location from the use of landowners' temples as centres of administration for their estates. This drew to them other temples, those of the popular nature gods, as communities collected about them. Then, under the Shang, a new scale of government begins to make itself felt; we find stamped-earth ramparts, specialized aristocratic and court quarters and the remains of large buildings. At Anyang, a Shang capital in about 1300 BCE, there were metal foundries and potters' kilns as well as palaces and a royal graveyard. By late Chou times, the capital Wang Ch'eng is surrounded by a rectangle of earth walls each nearly three kilometres long.

There were scores of cities by 500 BCE and their prevalence implies an increasingly varied society. Many of them had three well-defined areas: a small enclosure where the aristocracy lived, a larger one inhabited by

This 19th-century CE engraving depicts Confucius surrounded by his disciples. The master said, "Yu, do you want me to teach you what knowledge is? If you know something, you must state what you know. If you do not know something, you must confess that you do not know. That is knowledge." (*The Analects of Confucius*, II, 17)

specialized craftsmen and merchants, and the fields outside the walls which fed the city. A merchant class was another important development. It may not have been much regarded by the landowners but well before 1000 BCE a cowry shell currency was used which shows a new complexity of economic life and the presence of specialists in trade. Their quarters and those of the craftsmen were distinguished from those of the nobility by walls and ramparts round the latter, but they, too, fell within the walls of the city – a sign of a growing need for defence. In the commercial streets of cities of the Warring States Period could be found shops selling jewellery, curios, food and clothing, as well as taverns, gambling houses and brothels.

THE GROWING INDEPENDENCE OF THE NOBILITY

The heart of Chinese society, none the less, still beat to the slow rhythms of the countryside. The privileged class which presided over the land system showed unmistakable signs of a growing independence of its kings as the Chou period came to an end. Landowners originally had the responsibility of providing soldiers to the king and development in the art of war helped to increase their independence. The nobleman had always had a monopoly of arms; this was already significant when, in Shang times, Chinese weaponry was limited for the most part to the bow and the bronze halberd. As time passed, only noblemen could afford the more expensive weapons, armour and horses which increasingly came into use. The warrior using a chariot as a platform for archery before descending to fight the last stage of the battle on foot with bronze weapons evolved in the last centuries of the pre-Common Era into a member of a team of two or three armoured warriors, moving with a company of sixty or seventy attendants and supporters, accompanied by a battle-wagon carrying the heavy armour and new weapons like the cross-bow and long iron sword which were needed at the scene of action. The nobleman remained the key figure under this system as in earlier times.

As historical records become clearer, it can be seen that economic supremacy was rooted in customary tenure which was very potent and far reaching. Ownership of estates – theoretically all granted by the king – extended not only to land but to carts, livestock, implements and, above all, people. Labourers could be sold, exchanged, or left by will. This was another basis of a growing independence for the nobility, but it also gave fresh importance to distinctions within the landowning class. In principle, estates were held by them in

From the 1st millennium BCE, circular coins with a hole in the centre were common (see above), and they are still the standard type of coin used by the Chinese.

concentric circles about the king's own demesne, according to their closeness to the royal line and, therefore, according to the degree of closeness of their relations with the spirit world. By about 600 BCE, it seems clear that this had effectively reduced the king to dependence on the greatest princes. There appear a succession of protectors of the royal house; kings could only resist the encroachments of these oriental Bolingbrokes and Warwicks in so far as the success of any one of them inevitably provoked the jealousy of others, and because of the kingly religious prestige which still counted for much with the lesser nobility. The whole late Chou period was marked by grave disorder and growing scepticism, though, about the criteria by which the right to rule was recognizable. The price of survival for the princes who disputed China was the elaboration of more effective governments and armed forces, and often they welcomed innovators prepared to set aside tradition.

THE HUNDRED SCHOOLS ERA

In the profound and prolonged social and political crisis of the last, decaying centuries

of the Chou and the Period of Warring States (433–221 BCE), there was a burst of speculation about the foundations of government and ethics. The era was to remain famous as the time of the "Hundred Schools", when wandering scholars moved about from patron to patron, expounding their teachings. One sign of this new development was the appearance of a school of writers known as the "Legalists". They urged that law-making power should replace ritual observances as the principle of organization of the state; there should be one law for all, ordained and vigorously applied by one ruler. The aim of this was the creation of a wealthy and powerful state. This seemed to many of their opponents to be little more than a cynical doctrine of power, but the Legalists were to have important successes in the next few centuries because kings, at least, liked their ideas. The debate went on for a long time.

CONFUCIUS

IN THE DEBATE about the organization of the state, the main opponents of the Legalists were the followers of the teacher who is the most famous of all Chinese thinkers, Confucius. It is convenient to call him by that name, though it is only a latinized version of his Chinese name, K'ung-fu-tzu, and was given to him by Europeans in the seventeenth century CE, more than two thousand years after his birth in the middle of the sixth century BCE. He was to be more profoundly respected in China than any other philosopher. What he said – or was said to have said – shaped his countrymen's thinking for two thousand

Dating from the 3rd century BCE, these ancient Chinese bronze coins are in the shapes of a hoe and a knife.

years and was to be paid the compliment of bitter attack by the first post-Confucian Chinese state, the Marxist republic of the twentieth century CE.

THE PRECEPTS OF CONFUCIUS

Confucius came from a *shih* family. He was a member of the lesser nobility who had

This 16th-century CE ivory statue portrays Confucius. Even though sacred ceremonies were held in his honour, the great Chinese master considered himself to be a secular thinker, as opposed to a religious prophet. On one occasion he said, "If we know nothing about life how can we know anything about death?" (*The Analects of Confucius*, XI, 11)

spent some time as a minister of state and an overseer of granaries. When he could not find a ruler to put into practice his recommendations for just government he turned to meditation and teaching; his aim was to present a purified and more abstract version of the doctrine he believed to lie at the heart of the traditional practices and thus to revive personal integrity and disinterested service in the governing class. He was a reforming conservative, seeking to teach his pupils the essential truths of a system materialized and obscured by routine. Somewhere in the past, he thought, lay a mythical age when everyone knew his or her place and duty; to return to that was Confucius' ethical goal. He advocated the principle of order – the attribution to everything of its correct place in the great whole of experience. The practical expression of this was the strong Confucian predisposition to support the institutions likely to ensure order – the family, hierarchy, seniority – and due reverence for the many nicely graded obligations between people.

This was teaching likely to produce individuals who would respect the traditional culture, emphasize the value of good form and regular behaviour, and seek to realize their moral obligations in the scrupulous discharge of duties. It was immediately successful in that many of Confucius' pupils won fame and worldly success (though his teaching deplored the conscious pursuit of such goals, urging, rather, a gentlemanly self-effacement). But it was also successful in a much more fundamental sense, since generations of Chinese civil servants were later to be drilled in the precepts of behaviour and government which he laid down. "Documents, conduct, loyalty and faithfulness", four precepts attributed to him as his guidance on government, helped to form reliable, disinterested and humane civil servants for hundreds of years, even if not always with uniform success.

The style of the teachings of Confucius, who is depicted in this 18th-century CE portrait, is reflected in the maxim, "To learn without thinking is fatal but to think without learning is just as bad." (*The Analects of Confucius*, II, 15)

Mysticism and philosophy in ancient China

Various archaeological finds provide evidence that, at the time of the Shang and Chou dynasties, members of the royal family and the aristocracy believed in the power of dead ancestors and that this belief lay at the heart of their religion. The 6th century BCE, however, saw the appearance of the two philosophical trends that have dominated Chinese thinking to the present day: Confucianism and Taoism. Confucianism was the philosophy of social organisation, of common sense and practical knowledge. Taoism was the philosophy of the contemplation of nature, of tranquillity, and of eternal rebirth.

CONFUCIUS

Confucianism derives its name from K'ung-fu-tzu or Confucius (551–479 BCE). He was a social and moral reformer rather than a religious leader. His ideology was adopted by the ruling classes for 2,000 years and became the basis of Chinese philosophy.

Later, Meng-tzu or Mencius (4th century BCE) was to add to this doctrine the idea of humanity's benevolence and natural goodness. Hsün-tzu (3rd century BCE) attacked the doctrine of Mencius with its opposite, stating that human beings are evil and must be taught to follow the path of morality.

LAO TZU

Taoists believe Lao Tzu was the creator of Taoism. Thought to be a contemporary of Confucius, he was the legendary author of a book of aphorisms called *Tao-te Ching* (*The Classic of the Way and its Power*).

The philosophies of Confucianism, Taoism and Buddhism are often collectively referred to as the "three teachings".

THE THIRTEEN CLASSICS

Confucian texts were later to be treated with something like religious awe. His name gave great prestige to anything with which it was associated. He was said to have compiled some of the texts later known as the Thirteen Classics, a collection which only took its final form in the thirteenth century CE. Rather like the Old Testament, they were a somewhat miscellaneous collection of old poems, chronicles, early state documents, moral sayings and an early cosmogony called the Book of Changes, but they were used for centuries in a unified and creative way to mould generations of Chinese civil servants and rulers in the precepts which were believed to be those approved by Confucius (the parallel with the use of the Bible, at least in Protestant countries, is striking here, too). The stamp of authority was set upon this collection by the tradition that Confucius had selected it and that it must therefore contain doctrine which

digested his teaching. Almost incidentally it also reinforced still more the use of the Chinese in which these texts were written as the common language of Chinese intellectuals; the collection was another tie pulling a huge and varied country together in a common culture.

It is striking that Confucius had so little to say about the supernatural. In the ordinary sense of the word he was not a "religious" teacher (which probably explains why other teachers had greater success with the masses). He was essentially concerned with practical duties, an emphasis he shared with several other Chinese teachers of the fourth and fifth centuries BCE. Possibly because the stamp was then so firmly taken, Chinese thought seems less troubled by agonized uncertainties over the reality of the actual or the possibility of personal salvation than other, more tormented, traditions. The lessons of the past, the wisdom of former times and the maintenance of good order came to have more importance in it than pondering theological enigmas or seeking reassurance in the arms of the dark gods.

CHINESE THOUGHT

For all his great influence, Confucius was not the only maker of Chinese intellectual tradition. In part, the tone of Chinese intellectual life is perhaps not attributable to any individual's teaching, but shares something with other oriental philosophies in its emphasis upon the meditative and reflective mode rather than the methodical and interrogatory which is more familiar to Europeans. The mapping of knowledge by systematic questioning of the mind about the nature and extent of its own powers was not to be a characteristic activity of Chinese philosophers. This does not mean they inclined to other-worldliness and fantasy, for Confucianism was emphatically practical. Unlike the ethical sages of Judaism, Christianity and Islam, those of China tended always to turn to the here and now, to pragmatic and secular questions, rather than to theology and metaphysics.

This can also be said of systems rivalling Confucianism which were evolved to satisfy Chinese needs. One was the teaching of Mo-Tzu, a fifth-century thinker, who preached an active creed of universal altruism; people were to love strangers like their own kin. Some of his followers stressed this side of his teaching, others a religious fervour which encouraged the worship of spirits and had greater popular appeal.

TAOISM

Lao Tzu, another great teacher (though one whose vast fame conceals the fact that we know virtually nothing about him), was supposed to be the author of the text which is the key document of the philosophical system later called Taoism. This was much more obviously competitive with Confucianism, for it advocated the positive neglect of much that Confucianism upheld; respect for the established order, decorum and scrupulous observance of tradition and ceremonial, for example. Taoism urged submission to a conception already available in Chinese thought and familiar to Confucius, that of the Tao or "way", the cosmic principle which runs through and sustains the harmoniously ordered universe. The practical results of this were likely to be political quietism and non-attachment; one ideal held up to its practitioners was that a village should know that other villages existed because it would hear cockerels crowing in the mornings, but should have no further interest in them, no commerce with them and no political order binding them together. Such an idealization of simplicity and poverty was the very opposite of the empire and prosperity Confucianism upheld.

THE TEACHINGS OF MENCIUS

Still another and later sage, the fourth-century Mencius, taught people to seek the welfare of humanity. The following of a moral code based on this principle would assure that human beings' fundamentally beneficent natures would be able to operate; this was more a development of Confucian teaching than a departure from it. But all schools of Chinese philosophy had to take account of

This statuette depicts Lao Tzu, the legendary founder of Taoism, riding a buffalo.

Confucian teaching, so great was its prestige and influence. Eventually, with Buddhism (which had not reached China by the end of the Warring States Period) and Taoism, Confucianism was habitually referred to as one of the "three teachings" which were the basis of Chinese culture.

THE IMPORTANCE OF CONFUCIANISM

The total effect of the sages' teachings is imponderable, but enormous. It is hard to say how many people were directly affected by such doctrines, and in the case of Confucianism its great period of influence lay still in the remote future at the time of Confucius' death. Yet Confucianism's importance for the directing élites of China was to be immense. It set standards and ideals to China's leaders and rulers whose eradication was to prove impossible until our own day. Moreover, some of its precepts – filial piety, for example – filtered down to popular culture through stories and the traditional motifs of art. It thus further solidified a civilization many of whose most striking features were well entrenched by the third century BCE. Certainly its teachings accentuated the preoccupation with the past among China's rulers which was to give a characteristic bias to

A 3rd-century BCE terracotta figure, discovered near the mausoleum of the Qin emperor Shih Huang-ti. This is one of the few female effigies to have survived from that period, although thousands of male terracotta figures, forming the emperor's burial army, have been found.

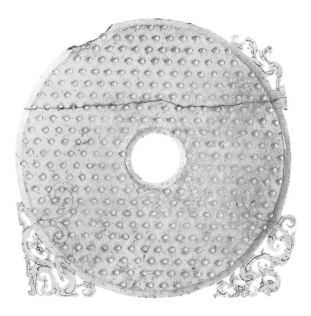

From the dawn of Chinese civilization jade disks, perhaps symbolizing the sky, have been produced. This example, carved in the 4th century BCE, demonstrates the masterful technique that Chinese craftsmen had acquired in working this precious material. The disk is pierced by a central hole representing an entrance to the void of timelessness.

Chinese historiography, and it may also have had a damaging effect on scientific enquiry. Evidence suggests that after the fifth century BCE a tradition of astronomical observation which had permitted the prediction of lunar eclipses fell into decline. Some scholars have seen the influence of Confucianism as part of the explanation of this.

ART AND ARCHITECTURE

China's great schools of ethics are one striking example of the way in which almost all the categories of her civilization differ from those of our own tradition and, indeed, from those of any other civilization of which we have knowledge. Its uniqueness is not only a sign of its comparative isolation, but also of its vigour. Both are displayed in its art, which is what now remains of ancient China that is most immediately appealing and

This bronze ritual vase dates from the late Shang period and was used to hold the fragrant wine that was offered to ancestors during sacred ceremonies. Thought to be from a Shang royal tomb, the vase is decorated with magical symbols, including dragon-like birds and animals and a large mask.

accessible. Of the architecture of the Shang and Chou, not much survives; their building was often in wood, and the tombs do not reveal very much. Excavation of cities, on the other hand, reveals a capacity for massive construction; the wall of one Chou capital was made of pounded earth thirty feet high and forty thick.

Smaller objects survive much more plentifully and they reveal a civilization which even in Shang times is capable of exquisite work, above all in its ceramics, unsurpassed in the ancient world. A tradition going back to Neolithic times lay behind them. Pride of place must be given none the less to the great series of bronzes which begin in early Shang times and continue thereafter uninterruptedly. The skill of casting sacrificial containers, pots, wine-jars, weapons, tripods was already at its peak as early as 1600 BCE. And it is argued by some scholars that the lost-wax method, which made new triumphs possible, was also known in the Shang era. Bronze casting appears so suddenly and at such a high level of achievement that people long sought to explain it by transmission of the technique from outside. But there is no evidence for this and the most likely origin of Chinese metallurgy is from locally evolved techniques in several centres in the late Neolithic.

None of the bronzes reached the outside world in early times, or at least there has been no discovery of them elsewhere which can be dated before the middle of the first millennium BCE. Nor are there many discoveries outside China at earlier dates of the other things to which Chinese artists turned their attention, to the carving of stone or the appallingly hard jade, for example, into beautiful and intricate designs. Apart from what she absorbed from her barbaric nomadic neighbours, China not only had little to learn from the outside until well into the historical era, it seems, but had no reason to think that the outside world – if she knew of it – wanted to learn much from her.

Thousands of life-size terracotta figures, such as this one, were found at the mausoleum of Shih Huang-ti, the Qin First Emperor. The figures are copies of the Chinese imperial army's soldiers at the end of the 3rd century BCE. This is a model of a rearguard archer in battle position. A cuirass of bronze plates protects his chest, shoulders and back.

3 THE OTHER WORLDS OF THE ANCIENT PAST

A herd of cattle, led by a drover, is depicted in this cave fresco in the Tassili mountains of the central Sahara. The image demonstrates that what is now a sun-scorched desert was a fertile region 6,000 years ago.

S O FAR IN THIS ACCOUNT huge areas of the world have hardly been mentioned. Although Africa has priority in the story of the evolution and spread of humanity and though the entry of men to the Americas and Australasia calls for remark, once those remote events have been touched upon, the beginnings of history focus attention elsewhere. The homes of the creative cultures which have dominated the story of civilization were the Near East and Aegean, India and China. In all these areas some

meaningful break in rhythm can be seen somewhere in the first millennium BCE; there are no neat divisions, but there is a certain rough synchrony which makes it reasonable to divide their histories in this era. But for the great areas of which nothing has so far been said, such a chronology would be wholly unrevealing.

This is, in the main, because none of them had achieved levels of civilization comparable to those already reached in the Mediterranean and Asia by 1000 BCE.

Remarkable things had been done by then in western Europe and the Americas, but when they are given due weight there still remains a qualitative gap between the complexity and resources of the societies which produced them and those of the ancient civilizations which were to found durable traditions. The interest in the ancient history of these areas lies rather in the way they illustrate that varied roads might lead towards civilization and that different responses might be demanded by different environmental challenges than in what they left as their heritage. In one or two instances they may allow us to reopen arguments about what constitutes "civilization", but for the period of which we have so far spoken the story of Africa, of the Pacific peoples, of the Americas and western Europe is not history but still prehistory. There is little or no correspondence between its rhythms and what was going on in the Near East or Asia, even when there were (as in the case of Africa and Europe though not of the Americas) contacts with them.

A giraffe has been discovered etched onto this rock wall in Twifelfontein, Namibia. Many similar examples of cave art, all of which are difficult to date, have been found in southwest Africa.

AFRICA

AFRICA IS A GOOD PLACE TO START, because that is where the human story first began. Historians of Africa, sensitive to any slighting or imagined slighting of their subject, like to dwell upon Africa's importance in pre-history. As things earlier in this book have shown, they are quite right to do so; most of the evidence for the life of the earliest hominids is African. With the Upper Palaeolithic and the Neolithic the focus moves elsewhere. Much continues to happen in Africa but the period of its greatest creative influence on the rest of the world is over.

CLIMATIC CHANGE

Why Africa's influence dwindles we cannot say, but there is a strong possibility that the primary force may have been a change of climate. Even recently, say in about 3000 BCE, the Sahara supported animals such as elephants and hippopotami which have long

Time chart (3500 BCE–450 BCE)				
		1300-800 BCE Urnfield cultures in Europe	1200–400 BCE Olmec culture in Mesoamerica	800–450 BCE Hallstatt Celtic culture in Europe
2000 BCE	1500 BCE		1000 BCE	500 BCE
	3500–1500 BCE Megalithic monuments in northern and western Europe		1200–200 BCE Chavin culture in Peru	

since disappeared there; more remarkably, it was the home of pastoral peoples herding cattle, sheep and goats. In those days, what is now desert and arid canyon was fertile savannah intersected and drained by rivers running down to the Niger and by another system seven hundred and fifty miles long, running into Lake Chad. The peoples who lived in the hills where these rivers rose have left a record of their life in rock painting and engraving very different from the earlier cave art of Europe which depicted little but animal life and only an occasional human. This record also suggests that the Sahara was then a meeting place of Negroid and what some have called "Europoid" peoples, those who were, perhaps, the ancestors of later Berbers and Tuaregs. One of these peoples seems to have made its way down from Tripoli with horses and chariots and perhaps to have conquered the pastoralists. Whether they did so or not, their presence and that of the Negroid peoples of the Sahara show that Africa's vegetation was once very different from that of later times: horses need grazing. Yet when we reach historical times the Sahara is already

desiccated, the sites of a once prosperous people are abandoned, the animals have gone.

THE PEOPLES OF AFRICA

It may be climatic change in the rest of Africa which drives us back upon Egypt as the beginning of African history. Yet Egypt exercised little creative influence beyond the limits of the Nile valley. Though there were contacts with other cultures, it is not easy to penetrate them. Presumably the Libyans of Egyptian records were the sort of people who are shown with their chariots in the Sahara cave-paintings, but we do not certainly know. When the Greek historian Herodotus came to write about Africa in the fifth century BCE, he found little to say about what went on outside Egypt. His Africa was a land defined by the Nile, which he took to run south roughly parallel to the Red Sea and then to swing west along the borders of Libya. South of the Nile there lay for him in the east the Ethiopians, in the west a land of deserts, without inhabitants. He could obtain no information about

Climatic changes in the Sahara

Ten thousand years ago, Mediterranean-type flora flourished in the Sahara desert region. The remains of several settlements reveal that fishing communities once existed on the shores of vast lakes. Tribes of farming settlers are also known to have lived in the central Sahara until c.2000 BCE. Progressive desertification brought an end to these ways of life.

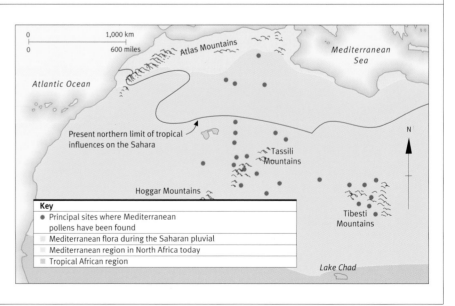

it, though a travellers' tale spoke of a dwarfish people who were sorcerers. Given his sources, this was topographically by no means an unintelligent construction, but Herodotus had grasped only a third or a quarter of the ethnic truth. The Ethiopians, like the old inhabitants of Upper Egypt, were members of the Hamitic peoples who make up one of three racial groups in Africa at the end of the Stone Age later distinguished by anthropologists. The other two were the ancestors of the modern San people (once derogatorily known as "Bushmen"), inhabiting, roughly, the open areas running from the Sahara south to the Cape, and the Negroid group, eventually dominant in the central forests and West Africa. (Opinion is divided about the origin and distinctiveness of a fourth group, the Pygmies.) To judge by the stone tools, cultures associated with Hamitic or proto-Hamitic peoples seem to have been the most advanced in Africa before the coming of farming. This was, except in Egypt, a slow evolution and in Africa the hunting and gathering cultures of prehistory have coexisted with agriculture down to modern times.

Fluctuations in the depth of Lake Chad

The changes that have taken place in the depth of Lake Chad in Africa from 10,000 BCE to the present demonstrate that levels of precipitation in the Sahara were much higher during the period 10,000–4000 BCE than they are today.

As the chart clearly shows, precipitation in the region reached its highest level 6,000 years ago. By the beginning of the Common Era, the volume of water contained in Lake Chad was little different from that to be found there now.

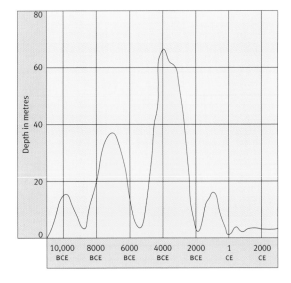

This chart illustrates the fluctuations that have occurred in the depth of Lake Chad over the last 12,000 years.

Rainfall is vital for the San who live in the Kalahari desert today, where for 10 months a year there may be no surface water. Like earlier African communities affected by the increasing aridity of their territory, the San are being forced to adapt to a changing environment. Their ancestors inhabited a large part of southern and eastern Africa 10,000 years ago.

THE SPREAD OF AGRICULTURE

The same growth which occurred elsewhere when food began to be produced in quantity soon changed African population patterns, first by permitting the dense settlements of the Nile valley which were the preliminary to Egyptian civilization, then by building up the Negroid population south of the Sahara, along the grasslands separating desert and equatorial forest in the second and first millennia BCE. This seems to reflect a spread of agriculture southwards from the north. It also reflects the discovery of nutritious crops better suited to tropical conditions and other soils than the wheat and barley which flourished in the Nile valley. These were the millets and rice of the savannahs. The forest areas could not be exploited until the coming of other plants suitable to them from Southeast Asia and eventually America. None of this happened before the birth of Christ. Thus was established one of the major characteristics of African history, a divergence of cultural trends within the continent.

THE KUSHITES

By the time of Christ's birth, iron had come to Africa and it had already produced the first exploitation of African ores. This occurred in the first independent African state other than Egypt of which we have information, the kingdom of Kush, high up the Nile, in the region of Khartoum. This had originally been the extreme frontier zone of Egyptian activity. After Nubia had been absorbed, the Sudanese principality which

This rock painting from Tassili in the Sahara desert depicts wounded warriors returning to camp and collapsing from pain and exhaustion. Various figures are shown going to their aid.

existed to its south was garrisoned by the Egyptians, but in about 1000 BCE it emerged as an independent kingdom, showing itself deeply marked by Egyptian civilization. Probably its inhabitants were Hamitic people and its capital was at Napata, just below the Fourth Cataract. By 730 BCE Kush was strong enough to conquer Egypt and five of its kings ruled as the pharaohs known to history as the Twenty-Fifth or "Ethiopian" Dynasty. None the less, they could not arrest the Egyptian decline. When the Assyrians fell on Egypt, the Kushite

This decorative jug, with handles and a spout, demonstrates the highly artistic quality of Chavin pottery.

dynasty ended. Though Egyptian civilization continued in the kingdom of Kush, a pharaoh of the next dynasty invaded it in the early sixth century BCE. After this, the Kushites, too, began to push their frontiers further to the south and in so doing their kingdom underwent two important changes. It became more Negroid, its language and literature reflecting a weakening of Egyptian trends, and it extended its territory over new territories which contained both iron ore and the fuel needed to smelt it. The technique of smelting had been learnt from the Assyrians. The new Kushite capital at Meroë became the metallurgical centre of Africa. Iron weapons gave the Kushites the advantage over their neighbours which northern peoples had enjoyed in the past over Egypt, and iron tools extended the area which could be cultivated. On this basis was to rest some three hundred years of prosperity and civilization in the Sudan, though later than the age we are now considering.

THE AMERICAS

IT IS CLEAR THAT THE HISTORY of humankind in the Americas is much shorter than that in Africa or, indeed, in any other part of the world except Australasia. Something like thirty thousand years ago, Mongoloid peoples crossed into North America from Asia. Over the next few thousand years they filtered slowly southwards. Cave-dwellers

This head is one of eight such colossal figures that have been found at a site at San Lorenzo, in Mexico. Between 1200 and 900 BCE, the site was an important Olmec ceremonial centre. These extraordinary heads, which are carved in basalt and weigh more than 20 tons each, are thought to depict Olmec rulers.

have been traced in the Peruvian Andes as many as eighteen thousand years ago. The Americas contain very varied climates and environments; it is scarcely surprising, therefore, that archaeological evidence shows there were almost equally varied patterns of life, based on different opportunities for hunting, food-gathering and fishing. What they learnt from one another is probably undiscoverable. What is indisputable is that some of these cultures arrived at the invention of agriculture independently of the Old World.

AGRICULTURE IN THE AMERICAS

Disagreement is still possible about when precisely the invention of agriculture happened in the Americas because, paradoxically, a great deal is known about the early cultivation of plants at a time when the scale on which this took place cannot reasonably be called agriculture. It is, nevertheless, a change which comes later than in the Fertile Crescent. Maize began to be cultivated in Mexico in about 5000 BCE, but had been improved by 2000 BCE in Mesoamerica into something like the plant we know today. This is the sort of change which made possible the establishment of large settled communities. Farther south, potatoes and manioc (another starchy root vegetable) also begin to appear at about this time and a little later there

A 1st-millennium BCE Olmec figure. The Mesoamerican artistic tradition began with the Olmec culture.

are signs that maize has spread southwards from Mexico. Everywhere, though, change is gradual; to talk of an "agricultural revolution" is even less appropriate in the Americas than in the Near East.

THE OLMECS

Farming, villages, weaving and pottery all appear in Central America in the second millennium BCE and towards the end of it come the first stirrings of the culture which produced the first recognized American civilization, that of the Olmecs of the eastern Mexican coast. It was focused, it seems, on important ceremonial sites with large earth pyramids. At these sites have been found colossal monumental sculpture and fine carvings of figures in jade. The style of this work is highly individual. It concentrates on human and jaguar-like images, sometimes fusing them. For several centuries after 800 BCE it seems to have prevailed right across Central America as far south as what is now El Salvador. But it retains its mystery, appearing without antecedents or warning in a swampy, forested region which makes it hard to explain in economic terms. We do not know why civilization which elsewhere required the relative plenty of the great river valleys should in the Americas spring from such unpromising soil.

Olmec civilization transmitted something to the future, for the gods of the later Aztecs were to be descendants of those of the Olmecs. It may also be that the early hieroglyphic systems of

The Chavin culture was the first major Andean culture. Its most important ceremonial centre was located at the site of the present-day Peruvian city of Chavin de Huantar. Supernatural creatures, such as the one shown above, decorated the outer walls of the site's ancient temple.

Central America originate in Olmec times, though the first survivals of the characters of these systems follow only a century or so after the disappearance of Olmec culture in about 400 BCE. Again, we do not know why or how this happened. Much further south, in Peru, a culture called Chavin (after a great ceremonial site) also appeared and survived a little later than Olmec civilization to the north. It, too, had a high level of skill in working stone and spread vigorously only to dry up mysteriously.

What should be thought of these early lunges in the direction of civilization is very hard to see. Whatever their significance for the future, they are millennia behind the appearance of civilization elsewhere, whatever the cause of that may be. When the Spanish landed in the New World nearly two thousand years after the disappearance of Olmec culture they would still find most of its inhabitants working with stone tools. They would also find complicated societies

This intricately decorated gold *lunula* (a crescent moon-shaped necklace) was found in Blessington in County Wicklow, Ireland. It dates from around 2000 BCE.

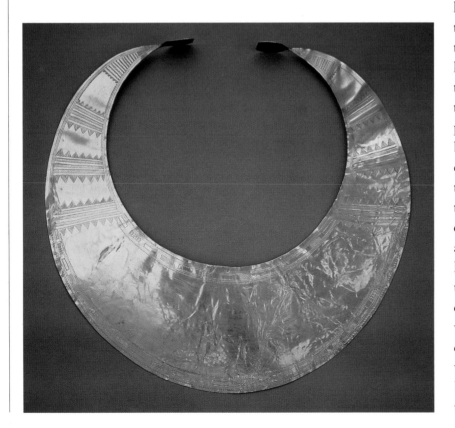

(and the relics of others) which had achieved prodigies of building and organization far out-running, for example, anything Africa could offer after the decline of ancient Egypt. It is clear only that there are no unbreakable sequences in these matters.

EUROPE

THE ONLY OTHER AREA where a startlingly high level of achievement in stone-working was reached was western Europe. This has led enthusiasts to claim it as another seat of early "civilization", almost as if its inhabitants were some sort of depressed class needing historical rehabilitation. Europe has already been touched upon as a supplier of metals to the ancient Near East. Yet, though much that we now find interesting was happening there in prehistoric times, it does not provide a very impressive or striking story. In the history of the world, prehistoric Europe has little except illustrative importance. To the great civilizations which rose and fell in the river valleys of the Near East, Europe was largely an irrelevance. It sometimes received the impress of the outside world but contributed only marginally and fitfully to the process of historic change. A parallel might be Africa at a later date, interesting for its own sake, but not for its positive contribution to world history. It was to be a very long time before men would even be able to conceive that there existed a geographical, let alone a cultural, unity corresponding to the later idea of Europe. To the ancient world, the northern lands where the barbarians came from before they appeared in Thrace were irrelevant (and most of them probably came from further east anyway). The north-western hinterland was only important because it occasionally disgorged commodities wanted in Asia and the Aegean.

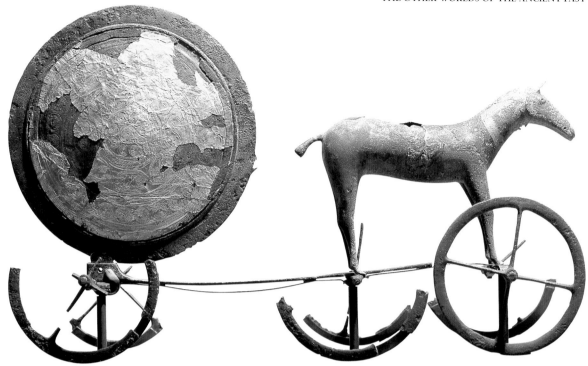

This figure, from Trudholm on the Danish island of Seeland, is one of the most important archaeological pieces from Bronze Age Europe. The figure represents a horse on a wheeled base pulling a disk, which is gold-plated on one side. It is thought that the object represents a mythical chariot carrying the sun across the sky.

THE TWO REGIONS WITHIN PREHISTORIC EUROPE

There is not much to say about prehistoric Europe, but in order to get a correct perspective, one more point should be made. Two Europes must be separated. One is that of the Mediterranean coasts and their peoples. Its rough boundary is the line which delimits the cultivation of the olive. South of this line, literate, urban civilization comes fairly quickly once we are into the Iron Age, and apparently comes by direct contact with more advanced areas. By 800 BCE the coasts of the western Mediterranean were already beginning to experience fairly continuous contact with the East. The Europe north and west of this line is a different matter. In this area literacy was never achieved in antiquity, but was imposed much later by conquerors. It long resisted cultural influences from the south and east – or at least did not offer a favourable reception to them – and it is for two thousand years important not for its own sake but because of its relationship to other areas. Its role was not entirely passive: the movements of its peoples, its natural resources and skills all at times impinged marginally on events elsewhere. But in 1000 BCE – to take an arbitrary date – or even at the beginning of the Common Era, Europe has little of its own to offer the world except its minerals, and nothing which represents cultural achievement on the scale reached by the Near East, India or China. Europe's age was still to come; hers would be the last great civilization to appear.

EARLY FARMING METHODS IN EUROPE

Civilization did not appear later in Europe than elsewhere because the continent's natural endowment was unfavourable. It contains a disproportionately large area of the world's land naturally suitable for cultivation. It would be surprising if this had not favoured an early development of agriculture and this the archaeological evidence shows. The relative ease of simple agriculture in Europe may have had a negative effect on social evolution; in the great river valleys men had to work collectively to control

One of the earliest European images of a plough appears in this cave etching from the Val Camonica region in the Italian Alps. The etching, which dates from c.3000 BCE, also depicts copper daggers, axes, animals and a solar disk.

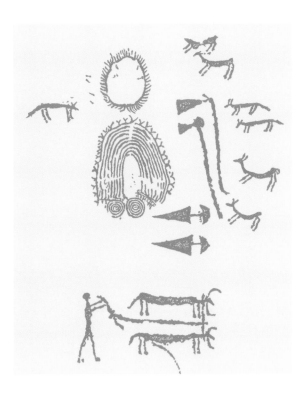

irrigation and exploit the soil if they were to survive, while in much of Europe an individual family could scratch a living on its own. There is no need to fall into extravagant speculation about the origins of western individualism in order to recognize that there is something very distinctive and potentially very important.

Recently, much earlier dates have been given to the evolution of prehistoric European farming – and metallurgy – than was once thought probable. Before 4000 BCE there were farming settlements in France and the British Isles. Perhaps a thousand years before this copper was being worked in the Balkans – some two thousand years before the appearance of recognizable civilization in Sumer. This early dating is not just of interest to scholars. It weakens the case once generally accepted, that Europe acquired its major cultural advances in prehistoric times by diffusion from the Aegean and Near East. The dates are now hard to fit. It seems certain that agriculture and copper-working were arrived at independently in Europe; this

emphasizes once again the relative isolation of the area in ancient times, though important transfers to it from the outside could take place. Though agriculture appeared there spontaneously, it seems that the most important cereals were brought in thousands of years later from the Near East.

THE DIVERSE PEOPLES OF EUROPE

Most of the northwestern and western parts of Europe were occupied in about 3000 BCE by peoples sometimes termed western Mediterranean, who were gradually squeezed out during the third millennium by Indo-Europeans from the east. By about 1800 BCE the resulting cultures seem to have fragmented sufficiently distinctly for us to identify among them the ancestors of the Celts, the most important of prehistoric European peoples, a society of warriors rather than traders or prospectors. They had wheeled transport. One enterprising group got to the British Isles and has some claim to being the first north-European sea-travellers. There is much disagreement about how far Celtic influence is to be traced, but it will not much disfigure the truth if we think of Europe divided in about 1800 BCE into three groups of peoples. The ancestors of the Celts then occupied most of modern France, Germany, the Low Countries and upper Austria. To their east were the future Slavs, to their north (in Scandinavia) the future Teutonic tribes. Outside Europe, in northern Scandinavia and northern Russia, are the Finns, a non-Indo-European race.

Except in the Balkans and Thrace, the movements of these peoples affected the older centres of civilization only in so far as they affected access to the resources of the areas into which they moved. This was above all a matter of minerals and skills. As the demands of the Near Eastern civilizations grew, so did Europe's importance. The first centre of metallurgy to develop there had been in the Balkans. Developments in southern Spain, Greece and the Aegean and central Italy followed by 2000 BCE. In the later Bronze Age, metal-working was advanced to high levels even in places where no local ores were available. We have here one of the earliest examples of the emergence of crucial economic areas based on the possession of special resources. Copper and tin shaped the penetration of Europe and also its coastal and river navigation because these commodities were needed and were only available in the Near East in small quantities. Europe was the major primary producer of the ancient metallurgical world, as well as a major manufacturer. Metal-working was carried to a high level and produced beautiful objects long before that of the Aegean, but it is possibly an argument against exaggerated awe about material factors in history that this skill, even when combined with a bigger supply of metals after the collapse of

Mycenaean demand, did not release European culture for the achievement of a full and complex civilization.

MEGALITHIC MONUMENTS

ANCIENT EUROPE HAD, OF COURSE, another art form which remains impressive. It is preserved in the thousands of megalithic monuments to be found stretching in a broad arc from Malta, Sardinia and Corsica, round through Spain and Brittany to the British Isles and Scandinavia. They are not peculiar to Europe but are more plentiful there, and appear to have been erected earlier – from about 3500 BCE – there than in other continents. "Megalith" is a word derived from the Greek for "large stone" and many of the stones used are very large indeed. Some of these monuments are tombs, roofed and lined with slabs of stone, some are stones standing singly, or in groups. Some of them are laid out in patterns which run for miles across country; others enclose small areas like groves of trees. The most complete and

Megalithic Europe

Megalithic constructions have been identified in numerous locations across Europe. Many megalithic monuments are located in Atlantic regions, such as Denmark, the western British Isles, Brittany, Portugal and Andalusia. This has fuelled speculation that the groups who erected these stones may have had contact with each other via the Atlantic Ocean.

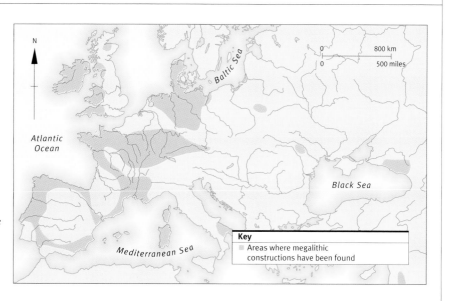

striking megalithic site is Stonehenge, in southern England, now dated to about 2000 BCE. What such places originally looked like is hard to guess or imagine. Their modern austerity and weathered grandeur may well be misleading; great places of human resort are not like that when in use and it is more likely that the huge stones were daubed in ochres and blood, hung with skins and fetishes. They may well often have looked more like totem-poles than the solemn, brooding shapes we see today. Except for the tombs, it is not easy to say what these works were for, though it has been argued that some were giant clocks or huge solar observatories, aligned to the rising and setting of sun, moon, and stars at the major turning-points of the astronomical year. Careful observation underlay such work, even if it fell far short in detail and precision of what was done by astronomers in Babylon and Egypt.

CONSTRUCTING THE MONUMENTS

Megalithic monuments represent huge concentrations of labour and argue for well developed social organization. Stonehenge contains several blocks weighing about fifty tons apiece and they had to be brought some eighteen miles to the site before being erected. There are some eighty pieces of stone there weighing about five tons which came 150 miles or so from the mountains of Wales. The peoples who put up Stonehenge without the help of wheeled vehicles, like those who built the carefully lined tombs of Ireland, the lines of standing stones of Brittany or the dolmens of Denmark, were capable of work on a scale approaching that of ancient Egypt, therefore, though without its fineness or any means of recording their purposes and

intentions except these great constructions themselves. Such skill, coupled with the fact of the monuments' distribution in a long chain within short distances of the sea, has suggested that their explanation might lie in what was learnt from wandering stonemasons from the East, perhaps from Crete, Mycenae, or the Cyclades, where the technique of dressing and handling such masses was understood. But recent advances in dating have once again removed a plausible hypothesis; Stonehenge was probably complete before Mycenaean times, megalithic

Europe's most extensive megalithic group was erected near Carnac, in Brittany, France. More than 3,000 menhirs (vertical stone blocks) were erected there, probably during the 2nd millennium BCE.

tombs in Spain and Brittany antedate the pyramids, and Malta's mysterious temples with their huge carved blocks of building stone were there before 3000 BCE. Nor do the monuments have to form part of any one process of distribution, even in the northwest. They may all have been achieved more or less in isolation, by four or five cultures made up of relatively small and simple agricultural societies who were in touch with one another, and the motives and occasions of their building may have been very different. Like its agriculture and metallurgy, prehistoric Europe's engineering and architecture arose independently of the outside world.

THE SHORTCOMINGS OF EUROPEAN CULTURES

For all their considerable achievements, the Europeans of ancient times seem strangely passive and unresisting when they finally appear in regular contact with advanced civilization. Their hesitations and uncertainties

stocks which would receive the impress of civilization later.

Only one group of western barbarians had a more positive contribution to make to the future. South of the olive-line an Iron Age people of central Italy had already during the eighth century BCE established trading contacts with Greeks further south in Italy and with Phoenicia. We call them Villanovans, after one of the sites where they lived. In the next two hundred years they adopted Greek characters for writing their language. By then they were organized in city-states, producing art of high quality. These were the Etruscans. One of their city-states would one day be known as Rome.

The Ile de Gavrinis dolmen, the interior of which is shown here, was constructed between 4000 and 3000 BCE in the Morbihan Gulf in Brittany, France. A dolmen is a burial chamber, consisting of large vertical stones supporting a horizontal top stone. The stone chamber is usually covered by a tumulus (mound) of earth.

may have resembled those of other primitive peoples meeting advanced societies at later dates – eighteenth-century Africans for example. But, in any case, regular contact only began shortly before the Common Era. Before then, the European peoples seem to have exhausted their energies in grappling with an environment which, though easily worked to satisfy modest needs, required the coming of iron to make it fully exploitable. Though far more advanced than their contemporaries in America, or in Africa south of the Nile valley, they never reached the stage of urbanization. Their greatest cultural achievements were decorative and mechanical. At best, in their metallurgy, the ancient Europeans serviced other civilizations' needs. Beyond that, they would only provide the

On the small island of Malta in the western Mediterranean, a number of megalithic temples have been preserved. They were built between 3500 and 2400 BCE, which makes them the world's oldest existing stone buildings. This is a view of the Ggantija Temple.

4 THE END OF THE OLD WORLD

Of what was going on in India and China and its importance for the future, the rulers of the Mediterranean and Near Eastern peoples knew hardly anything. Some of them, listening to traders, may have had a dim perception of a barbarian northern and northwestern Europe. Of what happened beyond the Sahara and of the existence of the Americas, they knew nothing. Yet their world was to expand rapidly in the first millennium BCE and, equally and perhaps even more obviously, it was to become more integrated as its internal communications grew more complex and efficient. A world of a few highly distinctive and almost independent civilizations was giving way to one where larger and larger areas shared in the same achievements of civilization literacy, government, technology, organized religion, city life and, under their influence, changed more and more rapidly as the interplay of different traditions increased. It is important not to think of this in terms too abstract or grandiose. It is not only registered by art and speculative thought, but also by much that is more down-to-earth. Small things show it as well as great. On the legs of the huge statues at Abu Simbel, seven hundred miles up the Nile, sixth-century Greek mercenaries in the Egyptian army cut inscriptions which recorded their pride in coming that far, just as two thousand five

Early civilizations in the Near East

Sumer, the oldest civilization in the Near East, emerged in the lower valley of the Euphrates and Tigris rivers and spread to the north of Mesopotamia. The Babylonian Empire encompassed the whole of Mesopotamia, while the Hittite Empire was founded in central Anatolia. In the 7th century BCE, the Assyrians controlled several of the earliest centres of civilization, from Sumer to Lower Egypt.

Key
- Sumer c.2100 BCE
- Babylonia under Hammurabi c.1750 BCE
- Hittite Empire c.1700 BCE
- Assyrian Empire c.650 BCE

This depiction of a shroud shows that during the last stage of its existence as an independent kingdom, when it was ruled by the Ptolemaic Dynasty, Egypt was strongly influenced by Greek culture. The figures of Anubis (right) and the other gods that surround the dead man are shown according to traditional Egyptian conventions; however, Osiris (left) and the deceased (centre) are of Greek inspiration.

hundred years later English county regiments would leave their badges and names cut into the rocks of the Khyber Pass.

THE LEGACY OF ANTIQUITY

There is no clear chronological line to be drawn in this increasingly complicated world. If one exists it has already been crossed several times before we reach the eve of the classical age of the West. The military and economic drive of the Mesopotamians and their successors, the movements of the Indo-Europeans, the coming of iron and the spread of literacy thoroughly mixed up the once-clear patterns of the Near East well before the appearance of a Mediterranean civilization which is the matrix of our own. Nevertheless, there is a sense in which it becomes manifest that an important boundary was crossed somewhere early in the first millennium BCE. The greatest upheavals of the *Völkerwanderung* in the ancient Near East were then over. The patterns set there in the late Bronze Age would still be modified locally by colonization and conquest, but not for another thousand years by big comings and goings of peoples. The political structures left behind from antiquity would be levers of the next era of world history in a zone which stretched from Gibraltar to the Indus. Civilization within this area would more and

Egypt was conquered in the 8th century BCE by the Nubian kingdom of Kush. This granite head depicts one of the Nubian pharoahs, King Taharqa (690–664 BCE).

more be a matter of interplay, borrowing and cosmopolitanism. The framework for this was provided by the great political change of the middle of the first millennium BCE, the rise of a new power, Persia, and the final collapse of the Egyptian and Babylonian-Assyrian traditions.

EGYPT IN DECLINE

The story of Egypt is the easiest to summarize, for it records little except decline. She has been called a "Bronze Age anachronism in a world that steadily moved away from her" and her fate seems to be explained by an inability to change or adapt. She survived the first attacks of the iron-using peoples and had beaten off the Peoples of the Sea at the beginning of the age of turmoil. But this was the last big achievement of the New Kingdom: thereafter the symptoms are unmistakably those of a machine running down. At home kings and priests disputed power while Egypt's suzerainty beyond her borders declined to a shadow. A period of rival dynasties was briefly followed by a reunification which again took an Egyptian army to Palestine, but by the end of the eighth century

Time chart (559 BCE–323 BCE)

559–529 BCE Reign of Cyrus II: Persian Empire founded		486–465 BCE Reign of Xerxes I: Second attack on Greece	
600 BCE	500 BCE	400 BCE	300 BCE
529–522 BCE Reign of Cambyses II: Conquest of Egypt	522–486 BCE Reign of Darius I: First attack on Greece	336–323 BCE Reign of Alexander the Great: Persian Empire brought to an end	

a dynasty of Kushite invaders had established itself; in 671 BCE it was ejected from Lower Egypt by the Assyrians. Ashurbanipal sacked Thebes. As Assyrian power ebbed, there was again an illusory period of Egyptian "independence". By this time, evidence of a new world towards which Egypt had to make more than political concessions can be seen in the establishment of a school for Greek interpreters and of a Greek trading enclave with special privileges at Naucratis in the Delta. Then again, in the sixth century, Egypt went down to defeat first at the hands of the forces of Nebuchadnezzar (588 BCE) and sixty years later, before the Persians (525 BCE), to become a province of an empire which was to set boundaries for a new synthesis and would for centuries dispute world supremacy with new powers appearing in the Mediterranean. It was not quite the end of Egyptian independence, but from the fourth century BCE to the twentieth century CE, she was to be ruled by foreigners or immigrant dynasties and passes from view as an independent nation. The last bursts of Egyptian recovery show little innate vitality. They express, rather, temporary relaxations of the pressures upon her which always, in the end, were followed by their resumption. The Persian threat was the last of these and was fatal.

PERSIA

ONCE AGAIN, THE STARTING-POINT is a migration. On the high plateau which is the heart of modern Iran there were settlements in 5000 BCE, but the word "Iran" (which does not appear until about 600 CE) in its oldest form means "land of the Aryans" and it is somewhere around 1000 BCE, with an irruption of Aryan tribes from the north, that the history of the Persian Empire begins.

In Iran, as in India, the impact of the Aryans was to prove ineffaceable and founded a long-enduring tradition. Among their tribes, two, especially vigorous and powerful, have been remembered by their biblical names as the Medes and Persians. The Medes moved west and northwest to Media; their great age came at the beginning of the sixth century, after they had overthrown Assyria, their neighbour. The Persians went south

This carved pillar stands among the ruins of the great Persian palace at Persepolis, which was built during the 5th century BCE.

towards the Gulf, establishing themselves in Khuzistan (on the edge of the Tigris valley and in the old kingdom of Elam) and Fars, the Persia of the ancients.

CYRUS

Oral tradition preserves a story of legendary kings more important for the light it throws on later Persian attitudes to kingship than as history. It was none the less from the Persian dynasty of the Achaemenids that there descended the first king of a united Persia – anachronistic though this term is. He was Cyrus, the conqueror of Babylon. In 549 BCE he humbled the last independent king of the Medes and thenceforth the boundaries of conquest rolled outwards, swallowing Babylon and advancing through Asia Minor to the sea, dropping down into Syria and Palestine. Only in the east (where he was eventually killed fighting the Scythians) did Cyrus find it difficult to stabilize his frontiers, though he crossed the Hindu Kush and set up some sort of supremacy over the region of Gandhara, north of the Jhelum.

This was the largest empire the world had seen until that time. Its style was different from its predecessors; the savagery of the Assyrians seems muted. At least brutality was not celebrated in official art and Cyrus was careful to respect the institutions and ways of his new subjects. The result was a diverse empire, but a powerful one, commanding loyalties of a kind lacking to its predecessors. There are some notable religious symptoms; the protection of Marduk was solicited for

In Pasargadae, Persia, stands the austere tomb of Cyrus the Great. The mortuary chamber, built from huge blocks, is raised on a stepped platform. According to one story, the body of Cyrus, who was killed in a border war, was never buried in the tomb.

On the rock wall of the Naqsh-i-Rustam pass, close to Persepolis, the burial places of four Persian kings have been excavated. Here, from left to right, are the tombs of Artaxerxes I, his father Xerxes I and his grandfather Darius I. The tombs' monumental façades recreate those of the great palace at Persepolis. The small entrances to the funeral chambers are located 50 ft (15 m) from the ground.

Cyrus's assumption of the Babylonian kingship and at Jerusalem he launched the rebuilding of the Temple. A Jewish prophet saw in his victories God's hand, named him the Lord's anointed and gloated over the fate of the old enemy, Babylon:

> "*Let now the astrologers, the stargazers, the monthly prognosticators, stand up, and save thee from these things that shall come upon thee.*"
>
> Isaiah xiv, 1, xivii, 1–13

IMPERIAL GOVERNMENT

Cyrus's success owed much to the material resources of his kingdom. It was rich in minerals, above all in iron, and in the high pastures of the valleys lay a great reserve of horses and cavalrymen. Yet it is impossible to resist the conclusion that sheer personal ability also counted for much; Cyrus lives as a world-historical figure, recognized as such by other would-be conquerors who were to strive in the next few centuries to emulate

This capital from Susa, the ancient Elamite city that Darius I turned into the administrative centre of his empire, is characteristic of Persian art. The upper part is formed by two bulls, whose backs are joined together in such a way that one beam rests on their heads and the other, perpendicular to the first, rests on their backs.

him. He based his government upon provincial governors who were the forbears of the later Persian satraps, and required from his subject provinces little beyond tribute usually in gold, which replenished the treasuries of Persia – and obedience.

Thus began the empire which, though with setbacks aplenty, provided for nearly two centuries a framework for the Near East, sheltering a great cultural tradition which grew to nourish itself both from Asia and Europe. Large areas knew longer periods of peace under it than for centuries and it was in many ways a beautiful and gentle civilization. Greeks were told already by Herodotus that the Persians loved flowers and there are many things we could do without more easily than the tulip, which we owe to them. Cyrus's son added Egypt to the empire; yet he died before he could deal with a pretender to the throne whose attempts encouraged Medes and Babylonians to seek to recover their independence. The restorer of Cyrus's heritage was a young man who claimed Achaemenid descent, Darius.

DARIUS

Darius (who reigned 522–486) did not achieve all he wished. His work, none the less, rivalled that of Cyrus. His own inscription on the monument recording his victories over rebels may be thought justified by what he did: "I am Darius the Great King, King of Kings, King in Persia", a recitation of an ancient title whose braggadocio he adopted. In the east the boundaries of the empire were carried further into the Indus valley. In the west they advanced to Macedonia, though they were checked there, and in the north Darius failed, as Cyrus before him, to make much headway against the Scythians. Inside the empire a remarkable work of consolidation was undertaken. Decentralization was institutionalized with the division of the empire into twenty provinces, each under a satrap who was a royal prince or great nobleman. Royal inspectors surveyed their work and their control of the machine was made easier by the institution of a royal secretariat to conduct correspondence with the provinces, and Aramaic, the old *lingua franca* of the Assyrian Empire, became the administrative language. It was well adapted to the conduct of affairs because it was not written in cuneiform but in the Phoenician alphabet. The bureaucracy rested on better communications than any yet seen, for much of the provincial tribute was invested in road-building. At their best these roads made it possible to convey messages at two hundred miles a day.

PERSEPOLIS

The great new capital at Persepolis, where Darius himself was buried in a rock tomb cut into the cliff face, was to have been a monument to his achievement. Intended as a colossal glorification of the king, it remains impressive even when it seems pompous. Persepolis was in the end a collective creation; later kings added their palaces to it and embodied in it the diversity and cosmopolitanism of the empire. Assyrian colossi, man-headed bulls and lions guarded its gates as they had done those of Nineveh. Up its staircases marched stone warriors bearing tribute; they are a little less mechanical than the regimented Assyrians of earlier sculpture, but only a little. The decorative columns recall Egypt, but it is an Egyptian device transmitted through Ionian stone-cutters and sculptors. Greek details are to be found also in the reliefs and decoration, and a similar mixture of reminiscences is to be found in the

The *apadana* (audience hall) in the palace of Persepolis was probably the citadel's largest audience chamber, with an interior of 4,300 sq yds (3,600 sq m). Its wooden ceiling was supported by 36 columns, which stood 65 ft (20 m) high and were crowned with decorated capitals.

Persepolis

A lion attacking a bull in a relief from the Persepolis citadel.

Darius I built his palace on a newly founded site, Persepolis, where his successors Xerxes I and Artaxerxes I would later add their own palaces. The remains of the city's residential district have not yet been found, but the imperial citadel has survived and is in extraordinarily good condition. There is an enormous terrace, 1640 ft (500 m) long by 985 ft (300 m) wide, which is raised 50 ft (15 m) above the ground on a brick platform. The terrace is reached by a monumental double stairway, the walls of which depict the majestic advance of long ranks of soldiers and tribute bearers. On the flat surface stand the ruins of various buildings. It took 60 years to construct this complex, between 500 and 440 BCE.

royal tombs not far away. They recall the Valley of the Kings in their conception while their cruciform entrances speak of something else. Cyrus's own tomb, at Pasargadae, had also been marked by Greek design. A new world is coming to birth.

PERSIAN CULTURE

Monuments such as those at Persepolis and Pasargadae fittingly express the continuing diversity and tolerance of Persian culture. It was one always open to influence from abroad and would continue to be. Persia took up not only the languages of those she conquered, but also sometimes their ideas. She also contributed. Vedic and Persian religion mingled in Gandhara, where stood the Indian city the Greeks called Taxila, but both, of course, were Aryan. The core of Persian religion was sacrifice and centred on fire. By the age of Darius the most refined of its cults had evolved into what has been called Zoroastrianism, a dualist religion accounting for the problem of evil in terms of the struggle of a good with an evil god. Of its prophet, Zoroaster, we know little, but it seems that he taught his disciples to uphold the cause of the god of light with ritual and moral behaviour; ahead lay a messianic deliverance, the resurrection of the dead and life everlasting after judgment. This creed spread rapidly through western Asia with Persian rule, even though it was probably never more than the cult of a minority. It would influence Judaism and the oriental cults which were to be part of the setting of Christianity; the angels of Christian tradition and the notion of the hellfire which awaited the wicked both came from Zoroaster.

THE INTERPLAY OF CIVILIZATIONS IN THE NEAR EAST

It is too early to speak of the interplay of Asia and Europe, but there are few more striking examples of the interplay of reciprocal influences which marks the end of the ancient world. We can mark an epoch. Right across the Old World, Persia suddenly pulled peoples into a common experience. Indians, Medes, Babylonians, Lydians, Greeks, Jews, Phoenicians and Egyptians were for the first time all governed by one empire whose eclecticism showed how far civilization had already come. The era of civilization embodied in distinct units of history was over in the Near East. Too much had been shared, too much diffused for the direct successors of the first civilizations to be any longer intelligible independent units of study. Indian mercenaries fought in the Persian armies; Greeks in those of Egypt. City-dwelling and literacy were widespread through the Near East. People lived in cities around much of the Mediterranean, too. Agricultural and metallurgical techniques stretched even beyond that area and were to be spread further as the Achaemenids transmitted the irrigation skill of Babylon to Central Asia and brought rice from India to be planted in the Near East. When Asian Greeks came to adopt a currency it would be based on the sexagesimal numeration of Babylon. The base of a future world civilization was in the making.

THE CLASSICAL MEDITERRANEAN: GREECE

MEASURED IN YEARS, more than half the story of civilization is already over by about 500 BCE. We are still nearer to that date than were the people who lived then to their first civilized predecessors. In the three thousand or so years between them, humanity had come a long way; however imperceptibly slow the changes of daily life in them had been, there is an enormous qualitative gap between Sumer and Achaemenid Persia. By the sixth century, a great period of foundation and acceleration was already over. From the western Mediterranean to the coasts of China a variety of cultural traditions had established themselves. Distinct civilizations had taken root in them, some firmly and deeply enough to survive into our own era. Some of them lasted, moreover, with little but superficial and temporary change for hundreds or even thousands of years. Virtually isolated, they contributed little to humanity's shared life outside their own areas. For the most part, even the greatest centres of civilization were indifferent to what lay outside their spheres for at least two thousand years after the fall of Babylon except when troubled by an occasional invasion. Only one of the civilizations already discernible by the sixth century BCE in fact showed much potential for expanding beyond its cradle – that of the eastern Mediterranean. It was the youngest of them but was to be very successful, lasting for over a thousand years without a break in its tradition. Even this is less remarkable than what it left behind, though, for it was the seedbed of almost all that played a dynamic part in shaping the world we still inhabit.

The Acropolis in Athens was badly damaged by a Persian attack in 480 BCE, but was rebuilt 40 years later under the supervision of Pericles. The Parthenon, built between 447 and 432 BCE, dominates this view of the famous ancient Greek monuments. On the left-hand side stands the Propylaia, the monumental entrance to the Acropolis, designed by Mnesicles and constructed between 437 and 432 BCE. The temple of Athene Nike, in front of the Propylaia, appears tiny in comparison to the mighty Parthenon towering above it.

1 *THE ROOTS OF ONE WORLD*

THE APPEARANCE OF a new civilization in the eastern Mediterranean owed much to older Near Eastern and Aegean traditions. From the start we confront an amalgam of Greek speech, a Semitic alphabet, ideas whose roots lie in Egypt and Mesopotamia, reminiscences of Mycenae. Even when this civilization matured it still showed the diversity of its origins. It was never to be a simple, monolithic whole and in the end was very complex indeed. For all that integrated it and gave it unity, it was always hard to delimit, a cluster of similar cultures around the Mediterranean and Aegean, their frontier zones blurring far outwards into Asia, Africa, barbarian Europe and southern Russia. Even when its boundaries with them were clear, other traditions always played upon Mediterranean civilization and received much from it.

This civilization also varied in time. It showed greater powers of evolution than any of its predecessors. Even when they had undergone important political changes their institutions remained fundamentally intact, while Mediterranean civilization displayed a huge variety of transient political forms and experiments. In religion and ideology, whereas other traditions tended to develop without violent changes or breaks, so that civilization and religion were virtually coterminous, the one living and dying with the other, Mediterranean civilization begins in a native paganism and ends by succumbing to an exotic import, Christianity; it was a revolutionized Judaism which produced the first world religion. This was a huge change and it transformed this civilization's possibilities of influencing the future.

THE MEDITERRANEAN CONTEXT

Of all the forces making for this culture's crystallization, the most fundamental was the setting itself, the Mediterranean basin. It was both a collecting area and a source; currents flowed easily into it from the lands of the old civilizations and from this central reservoir they also flowed back to where they came from and northwards into the barbarian lands. Though it is large and contains a variety of peoples, this basin has well-defined general characteristics. Most of its coasts are

The Greek sphinx was a fantastical creature, often depicted with a woman's head, a lion's body and the wings of a bird. The existence of this image in much Greek sculpture and pottery reveals the influence of the cultural traditions that preceded Greek civilization in the Near East and the Aegean.

narrow plains behind which quickly rise fairly steep and enclosing mountain ranges, broken by a few important river valleys. Those who lived on the coasts tended to look along them and outward across the sea, rather than behind them to their hinterland. This, combined with a climate they all shared, made the spreading of ideas and techniques within the Mediterranean natural for enterprising peoples.

The Romans, with reason, named the Mediterranean *Mare Magnum*, the Great Sea. It was the outstanding geographical fact of their world, the centre of classical maps. Its surface was a great uniting force for those who knew how to use it, and by 500 BCE maritime technology was advanced enough to make this possible, except in winter. Prevailing winds and currents determined the exact routes of ships whose only power was provided by sails or oars, but any part of the Mediterranean was accessible by water from any other. The upshot was a littoral civilization, with a few languages spoken widely within it. It had specialized trading centres, for exchanges of materials were easy by sea, but the economy rested firmly on the growing of wheat and barley, olives and vines, mainly for local consumption. The metals increasingly needed by this economy could be brought in from outside. The deserts to the south were held at bay further from the coast and for perhaps thousands of years North Africa was richer than it now is, more heavily wooded, better watered, and more fertile. The same sort of civilization therefore tended to appear all round the Mediterranean. The difference between Africa and Europe that we expect today did not exist until after 500 CE.

The rugged coast of the Aegean and its lack of flat land led many of the inhabitants of the ancient Greek peninsula to take to the sea. Technical prowess and knowledge of the sea currents and winds enabled them to open trade routes in the Mediterranean.

Born at the start of the 5th century BCE in Halicarnassus (a Greek colony on the coast of Asia Minor), Herodotus is considered by many to be "the father of history".

THE CULTURE OF THE CLASSICAL WORLD

THE OUTWARD-LOOKING PEOPLES of this littoral civilization created a new world. The great valley civilizations had not colonized, they had conquered. Their peoples looked inward to the satisfaction of limited aims under local despots. Many later societies, even within the classical world, were to do the same, but there is a discernible change of tempo and potential from the start, and eventually Greeks and Romans grew corn in Russia, worked tin from Cornwall, built roads into the Balkans and enjoyed spices from India and silk from China.

About this world we know a great deal, partly because it left behind a huge archaeological and monumental legacy. Much more important, though, is the new richness of written materials. With them, we enter the era of full literacy. Among other things, they include the first true works of history; important as were to be the great folk records of the Jews, the narrations of a cosmic drama built about the pilgrimage of one people through time, they are not critical history. In any case, they, too, reach us through the classical Mediterranean world. Without Christianity, their influence would have been limited to Israel; through it, the myths they presented and the possibilities of meaning they offered were to be injected into a world with four hundred years of what we can recognize as critical writing of history already behind it. Yet the work of ancient historians, important as it is, is only a tiny part of the record. Soon after 500 BCE, we are in the presence of the first complete great literature, ranging from drama to epic, lyric hymn, history and epigram, though what is left of it is only a small part – seven out of more than a hundred plays by its greatest tragedian, for example. Nevertheless, it enables us to enter the mind of a civilization as we can enter that of none earlier.

The world according to Herodotus

Herodotus, a contemporary of Pericles, visited Greece, Macedonia, Thrace, Ionia, Syria, Mesopotamia, Egypt and Cyrene, in North Africa. Everywhere he travelled, he carried out extensive research, guided by a profoundly critical attitude and a mistrust of existing fables and legends. The great wealth of knowledge that he amassed is contained in his series of nine books of history, which open with the sentence: "Herodotus of Halicarnassus here displays his inquiry, so that human achievements may not become forgotten in time, and great and marvellous deeds – some displayed by Greeks, some by barbarians – may not be without their glory; and especially to show why the two peoples fought with each other."

An extract from *The Histories* by Herodotus, translated by Aubrey de Sélincourt.

Map of the world according to Herodotus.

The laws of Gortys, carved on stone tablets on the island of Crete in the middle of the 5th century BCE, form the oldest Greek legal code. Some of the laws inscribed had been in use since the 7th century BCE.

CLASSICAL LANGUAGES

Even for Greece, of course, the source of much great literature, and *a fortiori* for other and more remote parts of the classical world, the written record is not enough on its own. The archaeology is indispensable, but it is all the more informative because literary sources are so much fuller than anything from the early past. The record they offer us is for the most part in Greek or Latin, the two languages which provided the intellectual currency of Mediterranean civilization. The persistence in English, the most widely used of languages today, of so many words drawn from them is by itself almost enough evidence to show this civilization's importance to its successors (all seven nouns in the last sentence but one, for example, are based on Latin words). It was through writings in these

languages that later people approached this civilization and in them they detected the qualities which made them speak of what they found simply as "*the* classical world".

DEFINING "CLASSICAL"

"Classical" is a perfectly proper usage, provided we remember that those who coined it were heirs to the traditions they saw in it and stood, perhaps trapped, within its assumptions. Other traditions and civilizations, too, have had their "classical" phases. What it means is that people see in some part of the past an age setting standards for later times. Many later Europeans were to be hypnotized by the power and glamour of classical Mediterranean civilization. Some contemporaries who lived in it, too, thought that they, their culture and times were exceptional, though not always for reasons we should now find convincing. Yet it *was* exceptional: vigorous and

This 1st-century Roman mural from Stabiae depicts ships in a well-established harbour, probably Stabiae or Puteoli. The busy trade routes that criss-crossed the Mediterranean Sea were vital to the development of the classical civilizations that grew up around its shores.

The theatre at the sanctuary of Asclepius in Epidaurus, in modern-day Turkey, dates from the 4th century BCE and is one of the best surviving examples of an ancient Greek theatre.

restless, it provided standards and ideals, as well as technology and institutions, on which huge futures were to be built. In essence, the unity later discerned by those who admired the Mediterranean heritage was a mental one.

THE LEGACY OF THE CLASSICAL WORLD

Inevitably, there was to be much anachronistic falsification in some of the later efforts to study and utilize the classical ideal, and much romanticization of a lost age, too. Yet even when this is discounted, and when the classical past has undergone the sceptical scrutiny of scholars, there remains a big indissoluble residue of mental achievement which

somehow places it on our side of a mental boundary, while the great empires of Asia lie beyond it. With whatever difficulty and possibility of misconstruction, the mind of the classical age is recognizable and comprehensible in a way perhaps nothing earlier can be. "This", it has been well said, "is a world whose air we can breathe."

The role of the Greeks was pre-eminent in making this world and with them its story must begin. They contributed more than any other single people to its dynamism and to its mythical and inspirational legacy. The Greek search for excellence defined for later peoples what excellence was and their achievement remains difficult to exaggerate. It is the core of the process which made classical Mediterranean civilization.

The culture of classical Greece spread across the Mediterranean to Asia Minor and was eventually carried even further east by the campaigns of Alexander the Great. The ruins of this 4th-century BCE temple of Athene are in Pirene, originally an early Ionian settlement, in present-day Turkey.

2 *THE GREEKS*

The oldest surviving Greek inscription is on this jug found in the tomb of Dipylon. It dates from c.750 BCE and is written from right to left. A transcription of the text suggests that the jug may have been a prize in a dance competition or a dedication for a banquet.

IN THE SECOND HALF of the eighth century BCE, the clouds which have hidden the Aegean since the end of the Bronze Age begin to part a little. Processes and sometimes events become somewhat more discernible. There is even a date or two, one of which is important in the history of a civilization's self-consciousness: in 776 BCE, according to later Greek historians, the first Olympian games were held. After a few centuries the Greeks would count from this year as we count from the birth of Christ.

GREEK-SPEAKING PEOPLES

The people who gathered for the first Olympian games and for later festivals of the same sort recognized by doing so that they shared a culture. Its basis was a common language: Dorians, Ionians, Aeolians all spoke Greek. What is more, they had done so for a long time; the language was now to acquire the definition which comes from being written down, an enormously important development, making possible, for example, the recording of the traditional oral poetry which was said to be the work of Homer. Our first surviving inscription in Greek characters is on a jug of about 750 BCE. It shows how much the renewal of Aegean civilization owed to Asia. The inscription is written in an adaptation of Phoenician script; Greeks

were illiterate until their traders brought home this alphabet. It seems to have been used first in the Peloponnese, Crete and Rhodes; possibly these were the first areas to benefit from the renewal of intercourse with Asia after the Dark Ages. The process is mysterious and can probably never be recovered, but somehow the catalyst which precipitated Greek civilization was contact with the East.

Who were the Greek-speakers who attended the first Olympiad? Though it is the name by which they and their descendants are still known, they were not called Greeks; that name was only given them centuries later by the Romans. The word they would have used was the one we render in English as "Hellenes". First used to distinguish invaders of the Greek peninsula from the earlier inhabitants, it became the name of all the Greek-speaking peoples of the Aegean. This was the new conception and the new name emerging from the Dark Ages and there is more than a verbal significance to it. It expressed a consciousness of a new entity, one still emerging and one whose exact meaning would always remain uncertain. Some of the Greek-speakers had

This bronze statue is known as the Piombino Apollo and dates from the 5th century BCE. The figure's serious expression, typical of the pre-classical period, contrasts with his classical-style headdress and the soft lines of his body. His left hand probably held an offering and on his left foot, in silver letters, there is a dedication to Athene.

in the eighth century BCE already long been settled and their roots were lost in the turmoil of the Bronze Age invasions. Some were much more recent arrivals. None came as Greeks; they became Greeks by being there, all round the Aegean. Language identified them and wove new ties between them. Together with a shared heritage of religion and myth, it was the most important constituent of being Greek, always and supremely a matter of common culture.

THE AEGEAN SETTING

Yet cultural ties were never politically effective. They were unlikely to make for unity because of the size and shape of the theatre of Greek history, which was not what we now call Greece, but was, rather, the whole Aegean. The wide spread of Minoan and Mycenaean influences in earlier civilized times had foreshadowed this, for between the scores of its islands and the shores which closed about them it was easy to voyage during much of the year. The explanation of the appearance of Greek civilization at all may well be largely a matter of this geography. The past certainly counted for something, too, but Minoan Crete and Mycenae probably left less to Greece than Anglo-Saxon England left to a later Great Britain. The setting was a much more important factor than history. It offered a specially dense distribution of economically viable communities using the same language and easily accessible

not only to one another but to older centres of civilization in the Near East. Like the old river valleys – but for different reasons – the Aegean was a propitious place; civilization could appear there.

Much of the Aegean was settled by Greeks as a consequence of limitations of opportunities

The discus thrower, a replica of the lost work of art sculpted by Myron in the mid-5th century BCE. The statue depicts one of the sports included in the ancient pentathlon. To win such a competition not only brought great honour to the athlete, but also to his family and his city. Sport played a major role in Greek culture and training prepared young men for war.

Time chart (776 BCE–404 BCE)			
776 BCE First Olympian games Date from which the Greek calendar begins		507 BCE Cleisthenes' political reforms in Athens	
700 BCE	600 BCE	500 BCE	
750–700 BCE Beginning of Greek colonization in the Mediterranean Greek alphabet emerges		500–479 BCE Median Wars: Greek victory over Persia	431–404 BCE Peloponnesian Wars between Athens and Sparta

which they found on the mainland. Only in very small patches did its land and climate combine to offer the chance of agricultural plenty. For the most part, cultivation was confined to narrow strips of alluvial plain which had to be dry-farmed framed by rocky or wooded hills; minerals were rare, there was no tin, copper or iron. A few valleys ran direct to the sea and communication between them was usually difficult. All this inclined the inhabitants of Attica and the Peloponnese to look outward to the sea, on the surface of which transport and communication was much easier than on land. None of them, after all, lived more than forty miles from it.

GREEK CIVILIZATION IS DIFFUSED

The region's predisposition to civilization was intensified as early as the tenth century by a growth of population which brought greater

The Greek world of the Aegean

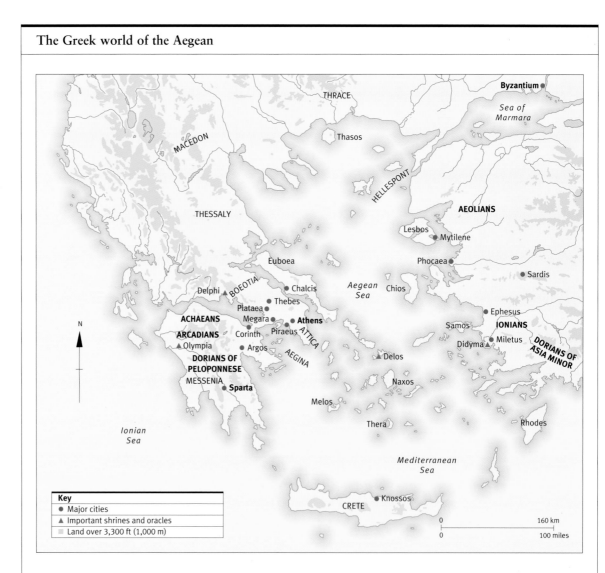

The Aegean coastline was dotted with Greek cities, most of which were involved in trading. Important settlements on the coast of Ionia, in Asia Minor, developed as a result of early emigration from mainland Greece, and Greek culture impregnated life in city-states throughout the Aegean. The remains of sanctuaries and oracles, which were attended by Greeks of all backgrounds, are scattered throughout the region.

In Greece narrow valleys and a lack of flat land made it difficult to produce large harvests. These unfavourable conditions drove many inhabitants of Peloponnesia and Attica to take to the Aegean Sea in search of new lands where they could settle.

pressure on available land. Ultimately this led to a great age of colonization; by the end of it, in the sixth century, the Greek world stretched far beyond the Aegean, from the Black Sea in the east to the Balearics, France and Sicily in the west and Libya in the south. But this was the result of centuries during which forces other than population pressure had also been at work. While Thrace was colonized by agriculturalists looking for land, other Greeks settled in the Levant or southern Italy in order to trade, whether for the wealth it would bring or for the access it offered to the metals they needed and could not find in Greece. Some Black Sea Greek cities seem to be where they are because of trade, some because of their farming potential. Nor were traders and farmers the only agents diffusing Greek ways and teaching Greece about the outside world. The historical records of other countries show us a flow of Greek mercenaries from the sixth century (when they fought for the

Egyptians against the Assyrians) onwards. All these facts were to have important social and political repercussions on the homeland, but before considering them there is much to be said about what kind of civilization it was which was being diffused in this way and was absorbing, by way of return, what others had to give.

LINGUISTIC IDENTITY

Quarrel violently among themselves though they did, and cherish the traditional and emotional distinctions of Boeotian, or Dorian, or Ionian though they might, the Greeks were always very conscious that they were different from other peoples. This could be practically important; Greek prisoners of war, for example, were in theory not to be enslaved, unlike "barbarians". This word expressed self-conscious Hellenism in its

This 6th-century BCE amphora reproduces a scene from the *Iliad*: the Greek warrior heroes Achilles and Ajax playing a game of dice. Although both players seem absorbed in the game, they hold their spears at the ready, prepared to resume battle against the Trojan enemy at any moment.

essence but is more inclusive and less dismissive than it is in modern speech; the barbarians were the rest of the world, those who did not speak an intelligible Greek (dialect though it might be) but who made a sort of "bar-bar" noise which no Greek could understand. The great religious festivals of the Greek year, when people from many cities came together, were occasions to which only the Greek-speaker was admitted.

RELIGION

RELIGION, TOO, WAS FUNDAMENTAL to Greek identity. The Greek pantheon is enormously complex, the amalgam of a mass of myths created by many communities over a wide area at different times, often incoherent or even self-contradictory until ordered by later, rationalizing minds. Some were imports, like the Asian myth of golden, silver, bronze and iron ages. Local superstition and belief in such legends was the bedrock of the Greek religious experience. Yet it was a religious experience very different from that of other peoples in its ultimately humanizing tendency. Greek gods and goddesses, for all their supernatural standing and power, are remarkably human. They express the human-centred quality of later Greek civilization. Much as it owed to Egypt and the East, Greek mythology and art usually presents its gods as better, or worse, men and women, a

The Greek pantheon

The Greeks were polytheists and depicted their gods as men and women, often moved by human passions. During the classical period, the twelve Olympian gods, who often had several personalities, were the most important deities. These Olympian gods were Zeus, Hera, Apollo, Artemis, Athene, Ares, Aphrodite, Demeter, Hephaestus, Poseidon, Hermes and Hestia. A large number of other lesser gods and local gods were also worshipped. Each city had a divine protector – Athene, goddess of intelligence, art and war, was the protector of Athens.

Rituals held in honour of the gods were usually carried out on open-air altars. These were placed in front of the doors of a sanctuary, in meeting places or in people's homes, rather than inside temples, which were used to house cult images of the gods.

This 5th-century BCE marble plaque depicts the birth of Aphrodite, as described in one of Homer's poems. The goddess of love emerges from the foaming sea, assisted by her servants, the Graces and the Seasons. Wife of the god Hephaestus, Aphrodite was the lover of both Ares and Adonis, mother of Eros and protector of the Trojan Paris, who abducted Helen.

world away from the monsters of Assyria and Babylonia, or from Shiva the many-armed. Whoever is responsible, this was a religious revolution; its converse was the implication that humans could be godlike. This is already apparent in Homer; perhaps he did as much as anyone to order the Greek supernatural in this way and he does not give much space to popular cults. He presents the gods taking sides in the Trojan war in postures all too human. They compete with one another; while Poseidon harries the hero of the *Odyssey*, Athene takes his part. A later Greek critic grumbled that Homer "attributed to the gods everything that is disgraceful and blameworthy among men: theft, adultery and deceit". It was a world which operated much like the actual world.

THE *ILIAD* AND THE *ODYSSEY* BY HOMER

The *Iliad* and the *Odyssey* have already been touched upon because of the light they throw on prehistory; they were also shapers of the future. They are at first sight curious objects for a people's reverence. The *Iliad* gives an account of a short episode from a legendary long-past war; the *Odyssey* is more like a novel, narrating the wandering of one of the greatest of all literary characters, Odysseus, on his way home from the same struggle. That, on the face of it, is all. But they came to be held to be something like sacred books. If, as seems reasonable, the survival rate of early copies is thought to give a true reflexion of relative popularity, they were copied more frequently than any other text of Greek literature. Much time and ink have been spent on argument about how they were composed. It now seems most likely that they took their present shape in Ionia slightly before 700 BCE. The Greeks referred to their author

without qualification as "the poet" (a sufficient sign of his standing in their eyes) but some have found arguments for thinking the two poems are the work of different men. For our purpose, it is unimportant whether he was one author or not; the essential point is that someone took material presented by four centuries of bardic transmission and wove it into a form which acquired stability and in this sense these works are the culmination of the era of Greek heroic poetry. Though they were probably written down in the seventh century, no standard version of these poems was accepted until the sixth; by then they were already regarded as the authoritative account of early Greek history, a source of morals and models, and the staple of literary education. Thus they became not only the first documents of Greek self-consciousness, but the embodiment of the fundamental values of classical civilization. Later they were to be even more than

Zeus was believed to be the father of all the gods as well as god of the sky. He used storms and lightning to show his wrath and administered justice on the earth and in heaven. He was the brother and husband of the goddess Hera and the father of countless heroes, the fruits of his relationships with goddesses and mortal women.

The *Odyssey*

"(Jove) saith, that here thou hold'st the most distrest
Of all those warriors who nine years, assail'd
The city of Priam, and, (that city sack'd)
Departed in the tenth; but, going thence,
Offended Pallas, who with adverse winds
Opposed their voyage, and with boist'rous waves.
Then perish'd all his gallant friends, but him
Billows and storms drove hither; Jove commands
That thou dismiss him hence without delay,
For fate ordains him not to perish here
From all his friends remote, but he is doom'd
To see them yet again, and to arrive
At his own palace in his native land."

An extract from Book V of the *Odyssey* by Homer, translated by William Cowper.

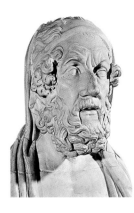

Homer, who was probably born in an Ionian city, lived between 750 and 650 BCE. The existing portraits of the poet, all of them imaginary, depict him as a blind, bearded figure. Homer's influence is omnipresent in Greek culture.

this: together with the Bible, they are the source of western literature.

THE OCCULT

Human though Homer's gods might be, the Greek world had also a deep respect for the occult and mysterious. It was recognized in such embodiments as omens and oracles. The shrines of the oracles of Apollo at Delphi or at Didyma in Asia Minor were places of pilgrimage and the sources of respected if enigmatic advice. There were ritual cults which practised "mysteries" which re-enacted the great natural processes of germination and growth at the passage of the seasons. Popular religion does not loom large in the literary sources, but it was never wholly separated from "respectable" religion. It is important to remember this irrational subsoil, given that the achievements of the Greek élite during the later classical era are so impressive and rest so importantly on rationality and logic; the irrational was always there and in the earlier, formative period with which this chapter is concerned, it loomed large.

SOCIETY AND POLITICS

THE LITERARY RECORD and accepted tradition also reveal something, if nothing very precise, of the social and (if the word is appropriate) political institutions of early Greece. Homer shows us a society of kings and aristocrats, but by his day this was already anachronistic. The title of king sometimes lived on, and in one place, Sparta, where there were always two kings at once, it had a shadowy reality which sometimes was effective, but by historical times power had passed from monarchs to aristocracies in

Mount Olympus, the highest mountain in Greece, was cited by Homer as the home of the Olympian gods. It is not surprising that the ancient Greeks installed their most important deities on the northern edge of the known world, on a mountain visible from the sea.

almost all the Greek cities. The council of the Areopagus at Athens is an example of the sort of restricted body which usurped the kingly power in many places. Such ruling élites rested fundamentally on land; their members were the outright owners of the estates which provided not only their livelihood but the surplus for the expensive arms and horses which made leaders in war. Homer depicts such aristocrats behaving with a remarkable degree of independence of his kings; this probably reflects the reality of his own day. They were the only people who counted; other social distinctions have little importance in these poems. Thersites is properly chastized for infringing the crucial line between Gentlemen and the Rest.

A military aristocracy's preoccupation with courage may also explain a continuing self-assertiveness and independence in Greek public life; Achilles, as Homer presents him, was as prickly and touchy a fellow as any medieval baron. To this day a man's standing in his peers' eyes is what many Greeks care about more than anything else and their politics have often reflected this. It was to prove true during the classical age when time and time again individualism wrecked the chances of cooperative action. The Greeks were never to produce an enduring empire, for it could only have rested on some measure of subordination of the lesser to the greater good, or some willingness to accept the discipline of routine service. This may have been no bad thing, but meant that for all their Hellenic self-consciousness the Greeks could not unite even their homeland into one state.

LIBERTY AND SLAVERY IN ANCIENT GREECE

Below the aristocrats of the early cities were the Other Ranks of a still not very complex society. Freemen worked their own land or

The Tholos at Delphi was located outside the grounds of the main sanctuary dedicated to the god Apollo. People came to Delphi from all over the Greek world to consult the oracle of Apollo on both political and private affairs.

sometimes for others. Wealth did not change hands rapidly or easily until money made it available in a form more easily transferred than land. Homer measured value in oxen and seems to have envisaged gold and silver as elements in a ritual of gift-giving, rather than as means of exchange. This was the background of the later idea that trade and menial tasks were degrading; an aristocratic view lingered on. It helps to explain why in Athens (and perhaps elsewhere) commerce was long in the hands of metics, foreign residents who enjoyed no civic privilege, but who provided the services Greek citizens would not provide for themselves.

A 6th-century BCE Athenian hydria. The decoration – a group of women, probably slaves, filling their hydrias at the fountain – alludes to the function of this jar, which was used to collect water. A number of monumental fountains, such as those shown here, were built in Athens during the 6th century BCE.

Slavery, of course, was taken for granted, though much uncertainty surrounds the institution. It was clearly capable of many different interpretations. In archaic times, if that is what Homer reflects, most slaves were women, the prizes of victory, but the slaughter of male prisoners later gave way to enslavement. Large-scale plantation slavery such as that of Rome or the European colonies of modern times was unusual. Many Greeks of the fifth century who were freemen owned one or two slaves and one estimate is that about one in four of the population was a slave when Athens was most prosperous. They could be freed; one fourth-century slave became a considerable banker. They were also often well treated and sometimes loved. One has become famous: Aesop. But they were not free and the Greeks thought that absolute dependence on another's will was intolerable for a free man though they hardly ever developed this notion into positive criticism of slavery. It would be anachronistic to be surprised at this. The whole world outside Greece, too, was organized on the assumption that slavery would go on. It was the prevailing social institution almost everywhere well into Christian times and it still survives. It is hardly cause for comment, therefore, that the Greeks took it for granted. There was no task that slavery did not sustain for them, from agricultural labour to teaching (our word "pedagogue" originally meant a slave who accompanied a well-born boy to school). A famous Greek philosopher later tried to justify this state of affairs by arguing that there were some human beings who were truly intended to be slaves by nature, since they had been given only such faculties as fitted them to serve the purposes of more enlightened individuals. To modern ears this does not seem a very impressive argument, but in the context of the way Greeks thought

Full-size bronze mirrors such as this one became fashionable at the end of the archaic age. In this example, the figurine shows the influence of oriental art. Only members of a wealthy family could afford to purchase such a luxury.

about nature and humanity there was more to it than simple rationalization of prejudice.

CONTACT WITH THE NEAR EAST

Slaves may and foreign residents must have been among the many channels by which the Greeks continued to be influenced by the Near East long after civilization had re-emerged in the Aegean. Homer had already mentioned the *demiourgoi*, foreign craftsmen who must have brought with them to the cities of the Hellenes not only technical skill but the motifs and styles of other lands. In later times we hear of Greek craftsmen settled in Babylon and there were many examples of Greek soldiers serving as mercenaries to foreign kings. When the Persians took Egypt in 525 BCE, Greeks fought on each side. Some of these men must have returned to the Aegean, bringing with them new ideas and impressions. Meanwhile, there was all the time a continuing commercial and diplomatic intercourse between the Greek cities in Asia and their neighbours.

GREEK ART

The multiplicity of day-to-day exchanges resulting from the enterprise of the Greeks makes it very hard to distinguish native and foreign contributions to the culture of archaic Greece. One tempting area is art; here, just as Mycenae had reflected Asian models, so the animal motifs which decorate Greek bronze work, or the postures of goddesses such as Aphrodite, recall the art of the Near East. Later, the monumental architecture and statuary of Greece was to imitate Egypt's, and Egyptian antiquities shaped the styles of the things made by Greek craftsmen at Naucratis. Although the

Most manual labour, both in the city and the countryside, was carried out by slaves, who also took care of domestic tasks. In Athenian comedies, the characters of the comic slave and servant were firm favourites. These small terracotta statuettes wearing grotesque masks were found in a 4th-century BCE Athenian tomb and depict actors dressed up for a performance.

The inside of a kylix (two-handled drinking vessel), depicting the god Dionysus who, after being captured by pirates, turned the mast of their ship into a vine and transformed the crew into dolphins.

final product, the mature art of classical Greece, was unique, its roots lie far back in the renewal of ties with Asia in the eighth century. What is not possible to delineate quickly is the slow subsequent irradiation of a process of cultural interplay which was by the sixth century working both ways, for Greece was by then both pupil and teacher. Lydia, for example, the kingdom of the legendary Croesus, richest man in the world, was Hellenized by its tributary Greek cities; it took its art from them and, probably more important, the alphabet, indirectly acquired via Phrygia. Thus Asia received again what Asia had given.

COMMERCIAL EXPANSION

Well before 500 BCE, Greek civilization is so complex that it is easy to lose touch with the exact state of affairs at any one time. By the standards of its contemporaries, early Greece was a rapidly changing society, and some of its changes are easier to see than others. One important development towards the end of the seventh century seems to have been a second and more important wave of colonization, often from the eastern Greek cities. Their colonies were a response to agrarian difficulties and population pressure at home. There followed an upsurge of commerce: new economic relationships appearing as trade with the non-Greek world became easier. Part of the evidence is an increased

circulation of silver. The Lydians had been the first to strike true coins – tokens of standard weight and imprint – and in the sixth century money began to be widely used in both foreign and internal trade; only the Spartans resisted its introduction. Specialization became a possible answer to land shortage at home. Athens assured the grain imports she needed by specializing in the output of great quantities of pottery and oil; Chios exported oil and wine. Some Greek cities became notably more dependent on foreign corn, in particular, from Egypt on the Greeks colonies of the Black Sea.

THE HOPLITES

Commercial expansion meant not only that land was no longer the only important source of wealth, but also that more men could buy the land which was so important in status. This began a revolution both military and political. The old Greek ideal of warfare had been single combat, a form of fighting natural to a society whose warriors were aristocrats, riding or driving to the field of battle to meet their equals, while less well-armed inferiors brawled about them. The new groups of wealthy men could afford the armour and arms which provided a better military instrument, the regiment of "hoplites", the heavy-armed infantry who were to be for two centuries the backbone of Greek armies and give them superiority. They would prevail by disciplined cohesion, rather than by individual derring-do.

The Greek hoplite wore helmet and body-armour and carried a shield. His main weapon was the spear, which he did not throw, but with which he thrust and stabbed in the mêlée which followed a charge by an ordered formation of spearmen whose weight gave it its effect. Such tactics could work only on relatively level ground, but it was such ground that was usually being contested in Greek wars, for the agriculture on which a Greek city depended could be devastated by seizure of the little plains of the valley floor where most of its crops were grown. On such terrain, the hoplites would charge as a mass, with the aim of sweeping away defenders by their impact. They depended completely on their power to act as a disciplined unit. This both maximized the effect of the charge and enabled them to prevail in the hand-to-hand fighting which followed, because each hoplite had to rely for protection on his right-hand side by the shield of his neighbour. To keep an ordered line was therefore crucial. The Spartans were in particular admired for their expertise in performing the preliminary evolutions which preceded such an encounter and for retaining cohesion as a group once the scrimmage had begun.

The ability to act collectively was the heart of the new warfare. Though bigger numbers now took part in battles, numbers were no longer all that counted, as three centuries of Greek success against Asian armies were to prove. Discipline and tactical skill began to matter more and they implied some sort of regular training, as well as a social widening of the warrior group. More men thus came to share in the power which comes from a near-monopoly of the means of exercising force.

CITY-STATES

THE DEVELOPMENT of a highly-trained army was not the only crucial innovation of these years. It was then, too, that the Greeks invented politics; the notion of running collective concerns by discussion of possible choices in a public setting is theirs. The magnitude of what they did lives on in the language we still use, for "politics" and "political" are terms derived from the Greek word for city, *polis*. This was the framework of Greek life. It was much more than a mere agglomeration of people living in the same place for economic reasons. That it was more is shown by another Greek turn of speech:

This funerary stele depicts a Greek hoplite. He wears a short tunic allowing free movement of the legs. His chest is protected by a metal or leather breastplate. On his head he wears a raised Corinthian-style helmet, part of which has been lost.

The decoration of this 7th-century BCE Corinthian jug depicts a group of horsemen taking part in a hunt. As neither saddle nor stirrups were used in Greece, the riders are mounted bareback. The cavalry played only a small role in the army and was never significant in attack; it was used to explore the terrain, to protect the army's flanks and to hound a retreating enemy.

This marble statue comes from an Athenian tomb and is a grave marker, or *kouros*. Made in about 530 BCE, it is a good example of how, as late as the 6th century BCE, Greek sculpture retained features from Egyptian art, including the rigidity and marked frontality of the body.

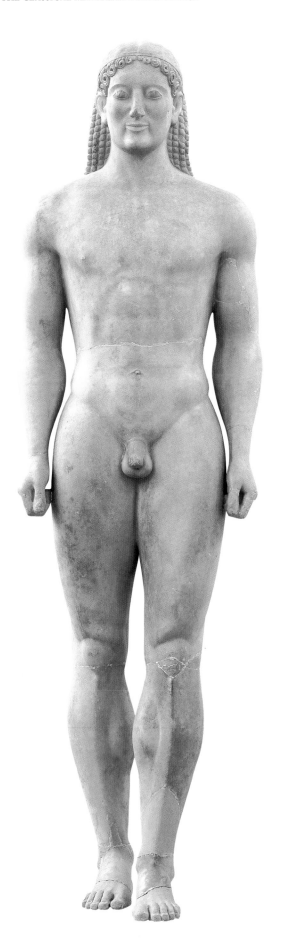

they did not speak of Athens doing this, or Thebes doing that, but of the Athenians and the Thebans. Bitterly divided though it might often be, the *polis* – or, as for convenience it can be called, the city-state – was a community, a body of men conscious of shared interests and common goals.

Such collective agreement was the essence of the city-state; those who did not like the institutions of the one they lived in could look for alternatives elsewhere. This helped to produce a high degree of cohesiveness, but also a narrowness; the Greeks never long transcended the passion for local autonomy (another Greek word) and the city-state characteristically looked outwards defensively and distrustfully. Gradually, it acquired its protecting gods, its festivals and its liturgical drama, which connected living people with the past and educated them in its traditions and laws. Thus it came to be an organism living in time, spanning generations. But at its root lay the hoplite ideal of disciplined, cooperative action in which men stood shoulder to shoulder with their neighbours, relying on them to support them in the common cause. In early days the citizen body – those, that is to say, who constituted the politically effective community – was confined to the hoplites, those who could afford to take their place in the ranks on which the defence of the city-state depended. It is not surprising that in later times Greek reformers who were worried about the results of political extremism would often turn hopefully to the hoplite class when looking for a stable, settled foundation for the *polis*.

At the roots of city-states lay also other facts: geography, economics, kinship. Many of them grew up on very ancient sites, settled in Mycenaean times; others were newer, but almost always the territory of a city-state was one of the narrow valleys which could provide just enough for its maintenance. A few

Greek Coins

The development of commerce in Greek cities stimulated the introduction of coins, probably around the mid-6th century BCE. We know that the first coins minted in Greece were made in Aegina, where silver, regularly brought from Siphnos, was used to produce the famous "silver turtles". A large variety of coins existed in the Greek world and the capacity to mint was seen as a sign of independence. Usually made of silver, the coins bore drawings and inscriptions showing the emblem of the city.

Greek coins dating from the 6th–4th centuries BCE – above: silver tetradrachma; right: silver stater from Poseidonia; far right: silver coin from Leontini.

were luckier: Sparta sat in a broad valley. A few were specially handicapped: the soil of Attica was poor and Athens would have to feed its citizens on imported grain in consequence. Dialect intensified the sense of independence latent in the mountains separating a city from its neighbours. In it was preserved a sense of common tribal origin which lived on in the great public cults.

CITIZENSHIP

By the beginning of historical times, intense feelings of community and individuality had already been generated which made it virtually impossible for Greeks to transcend the city-state: a few shadowy leagues and confederations did not count for much. Within the city the involvement of citizens in its life was close; we might find it excessive. Yet because of its scale the city-state could do without elaborate bureaucracies; the citizen body, always much smaller than the whole population, could always assemble at one meeting place. There was no likelihood that a city-state could or would aspire to a minute bureaucratic regulation of affairs; anything

like this would probably have been beyond the capacity of its institutions. If we judge by the evidence of Athens, the state of which we know most because it recorded so much in stone, the distinction between administration, judgment and law-making was not as we know it; as in the Europe of the Middle Ages, an executive act might be clothed as a decision of a court interpreting established law. Law-courts were, formally speaking, only sections of the assembly of the citizens.

The size and qualification of the membership of this body determined the

The wealthy city of Corinth produced an enormous amount of pottery for trade. The decoration of Corinthian pieces such as these often reflected the influence of the Near East, depicting fantastic animals, probably inspired by imported textiles.

constitutional character of the state. Upon it depended, more or less, the authorities of day-to-day government, whether magistrates or courts. There was nothing like the modern permanent civil service. True, it is still risky to generalize about such matters. There were over a hundred and fifty city-states and about many of them we know nothing; of most of the rest we know only a little. Obviously there were important differences between the ways in which they ran their affairs; in the fourth century BCE, Aristotle made a great collection of their constitutions and there would not have been much point in a political scientist doing this unless they were significantly different from one another. But the detail of what went on is hard to discern, even in the few cases where we have good information.

In the year 514 BCE, Hipparchus, son and successor of the Athenian tyrant Pisistratus, was killed by the tyrannicides Harmodius and Aristogeiton. After the fall of the Athenian tyranny in 510 BCE, their deed was extolled in this bronze sculpture.

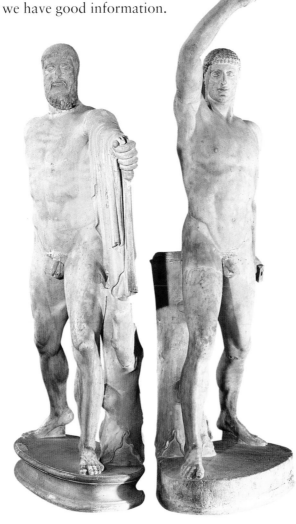

TYRANTS

The origins of Greek political forms are usually buried in legends as informative as the story of Hengist and Horsa is to the historian of England. Even Homer is unhelpful about the city-state; he hardly mentions it because his subject is warrior bands. Yet when the historical age dawns the city-state is there, ruled by aristocracies. The forces which determined the broad lines of its later evolution have already been touched upon. New wealth meant new men, and the new men battered away at the existing élites to get admission to citizenship. The aristocracies which had supplanted the kings themselves became objects of rivalry and attack. The new men sought to replace them by governments less respectful of traditional interests; the result was an age of rulers the Greeks called tyrants. They were often moneyed, but their justification was their popularity; they were strong men who set aside the aristocracies. The later sinister connotations of the word "tyrant" did not then exist; many tyrants must have seemed benevolent despots. They brought peace after social struggles probably intensified by a new crisis arising from pressure on land. Peace favoured economic growth, as did the usually good relations the tyrants enjoyed with one another. The seventh century was their golden age. Yet the institution did not long survive. Few tyrannies lasted two generations. In the sixth century the current turned almost everywhere towards collective government; oligarchies, constitutional governments, even incipient democracies began to emerge.

ATHENS

Athens was an outstanding example of this process. For a long time it seems that Attica, though poor, had sufficient land for Athens to escape the social pressures which in other states led to the colonization movement. In other ways, too, her economy early reflected a special vigour; even in the eighth century her pottery suggests that Athens was something of a commercial and artistic leader. In the sixth, though, she too was racked by conflict between rich and poor. A soon legendary lawgiver, Solon, forbade the enslavement of debtors by wealthy creditors (which had the effect of leading men to turn to greater dependence on chattel slaves, since debt bondage could no longer guarantee a labour force). Solon also encouraged farmers to specialize. Oil and wine (and their containers) became staple Athenian exports and grain was kept at home. Simultaneously, a series of reforms (also attributed to Solon) gave to the newly enriched equality with the old landed class and provided for a new popular council to prepare business for the *ecclesia*, the general assembly of all citizens.

Such changes did not at once quiet Athens' divisions. An age of tyrants only closed with the expulsion of the last in 510 BCE. Then there at last began to operate the institutions whose paradoxical outcome was to be the most democratic government in Greece, though one over a state which held more slaves than any other. All political decisions were taken in principle by majority vote of the *ecclesia* (which also elected the important magistrates and military commanders). Ingenious arrangements provided for the organization of the citizens in units which would prevent the emergence of sectional factions representing city-dwellers as against farmers or merchants. It was the beginning of a great age, one of prosperity, when Athens would consciously foster festivals and cults looking beyond the city and offered something to all Greeks. This was something of a bid for leadership.

SPARTA

Much has long been made of the contrast between Athens and her great rival, Sparta.

Every four years the Great Panathenaeas was held in Athens. This civic celebration in honour of the goddess Athene consisted of four days of athletic contests and festivities. The entire Athenian community also participated in a solemn procession to the Acropolis, bearing a new robe for the huge statue of Athene. The sculptor Phidias depicted the procession in his decorations for the frieze at the Parthenon, from which this fragment is taken.

Unlike Athens, Sparta met the pressures upon her not by modifying her institutions but by resisting change. She embodied the most conservative approach to the problem, solving it for a long time by rigid social discipline at home and by conquest among her neighbours which allowed her to meet the demand for land at others' expense. A very early consequence was a fossilizing of the social structure. So tradition-bound was she that it was alleged that her legendary law-giver, Lycurgus, had even forbidden her to write down her laws; they were driven home in the minds of the Spartiates by a rigorous training all undergone in youth, boys and girls alike.

Sparta had no tyrants. Her effective government appears to have been shared between a council of old men and five magistrates called "ephors", while the two hereditary kings had special military powers.

These oligarchs were in the last resort answerable to the assembly of the Spartiates (of whom, according to Herodotus, there were early in the fifth century about five thousand). Sparta was, therefore, a large aristocracy whose origin, ancient writers agreed, was the hoplite class. Society remained agricultural; no commercial class was allowed to appear and when the rest of Greece took up the use of money, around 600 BCE, Sparta stood out and permitted only an iron currency for internal use. Spartiates were not supposed to own silver or gold until the fourth century. Sparta even stood aside from the colonizing movement; she launched only one enterprise of this sort.

This produced a sort of militarized egalitarianism often admired by later puritans, and an atmosphere strongly suggestive, for good and ill, of the aspirations of the more

A bronze statuette of a Spartan wearing a large cloak. His long curls hang down under his helmet, to which a plume is attached. The statuette dates from approximately 500 BCE.

old-fashioned English public school. Though the passing of time and the position of kings slightly softened their practice, Spartiates knew no great distinctions of wealth or comfort. Until well into classical times they avoided dressing differently and ate at communal messes. Their conditions of life were, in a word, "spartan", reflecting the idealization of military virtues and strict discipline. The details are often strikingly unpleasant as well as curious. Marriage, for example, was a ceremony for which the bride's hair was cropped and she was dressed as a boy. It was followed by a simulated rape, after which the couple did not live together, the man continuing to live with his companions in a male dormitory and eating in messes with them. It is interesting that Sparta exported nursemaids to other Greek states (later parallels will again occur to the reader). She had no artistic or cultural achievement to speak of and her internal politics remain mysterious.

Possibly Spartan politics were simplified or muted by Sparta's gravest problem, the division between the citizen commune and the rest. The bulk of the inhabitants of the Spartan state were not citizens. Some were freemen, but most were helots, serf-like workers bound to the land who shared with the free peasants the task of producing the food consumed at the Spartiates' communal meals. Originally the helot population may have been the native population enslaved by the Dorian invasions, but they were like later serfs in being tied to land rather than being the chattels of individual owners. Certainly their number was later swollen by conquest, above all by the annexation in the eighth century BCE of the plain of Messenia, which disappeared from Greek history as an independent state for more than three hundred years. As a result, a cloud hung over the Spartan achievement – the fear of a helot revolt – and it was remarked by other

Greeks. It hobbled the Spartans in their relations with other states. Increasingly they feared to have their army abroad lest its absence should tempt revolt at home. Sparta was always on sentry-go and the feared enemy was at home.

THE GREEK ACHIEVEMENT

Sparta and Athens were to quarrel fatally in the fifth century and this has led them to be seen as always the poles of the political world of ancient Greece. They were not, of course, the only models available, and herein lies one of the secrets of the Greek achievement. It would draw upon a richness of political experience and data far greater than anything seen in the world until this time. This experience would provide the first systematic reflexions upon the great problems of law,

Solon, born in about 639 BCE, was the first important reformer of the Athenian constitution. He eliminated the punishment of slavery for debt from the statute book and worked to further democratize Athenian institutions.

duty, and obligation which have exercized people's minds ever since, largely in terms set by the classical Greeks. In pre-classical times, speculation on such themes is almost nonexistent. The weight of custom and the limitations of local experience sufficiently explain this.

COLONIZATION

The city-state was the shared inheritance and experience of the Greeks, but they knew of other types of political organization through contacts made in the course of trade and because of the exposed nature of many of their own settlements. The Greek world had frontier regions where conflict was likely. In the west they once seemed to be pushing ahead in an almost limitless expansion, but two centuries of striking advance came to an end round about

Types of pottery

The earliest Greek city-states developed the manufacture of pottery for exportation, as containers for commercial goods as well as for domestic and funerary purposes. Gradually, the shapes of Greek pottery objects evolved and the style of decoration used allows archaeologists to distinguish both the period and the geographical origin of a piece.

Some of the most common types of containers: (1) Amphorae, large pieces which contained wine and oil; (2) Kraters, in which wine and water were mixed to serve at banquets; (3) Oinochoes, wine jugs with a trefoil mouth to help pouring; (4) Jugs and cups for serving wine; (5) Arybaloi, small jars of oriental origin used to contain the ointments used by athletes; and (6 and 7) Lekythoi, small oil jars used to contain offerings to the dead.

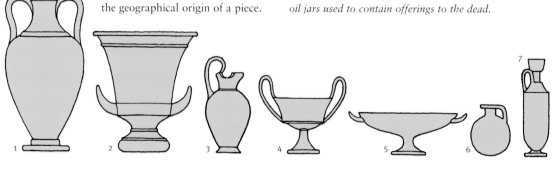

The Doric-style Temple of Concord in Agrigento, Sicily, was erected around 430 BCE. Because it was converted into a Christian church at the end of the 6th century CE, this is one of the best-preserved ancient Greek buildings.

550 BCE, when Carthaginian and Etruscan power prescribed a limit. The first settlements – once again, at sites sometimes used centuries earlier by Minoans and Mycenaeans – show that trade mattered as much as agriculture in their foundation. Their main strength lay in Sicily and in southern Italy, an area significantly to be called Magna Graecia in later classical times. The richest of these colonies was Syracuse, founded by Corinthians in 733 BCE and eventually the dominating Greek state in the west. It had the best harbour in Sicily. Beyond this colonial area, settlements were made in Corsica and southern France (at Massilia, the later Marseilles) while some Greeks went to live among the Etruscans and Latins of central Italy. Greek products have turned up even as far afield as Sweden and Greek style has been seen in sixth-century fortification in Bavaria. More impalpable influence is hard to pin down, but a Roman historian believed that Greek example first civilized the barbarians of what was later to be France and set them not only to tilling their fields, but to cultivating the vine. If so, posterity owes Greek commerce a debt indeed.

GREEK ENEMIES

The Greeks' vigorous expansion seems to have provoked Phoenician envy and imitation. It led the Phoenicians to found Carthage and the Carthaginians to seize footholds in western Sicily. Eventually they were able to close down Greek trade in Spain. Yet they could not turn the Greek settlers out of Sicily any more than the Etruscans could drive them from Italy. The decisive battle in which the Syracusans routed a Carthaginian force was in 480 BCE.

This was a date of yet greater significance for Greek relations with Asia, where the Greek cities of Asia Minor had often been at loggerheads with their neighbours. They had suffered much from the Lydians until they came to terms with the Lydian king, Croesus of legendary wealth, and paid him tribute. Before this, Greece already influenced Lydian

The colony of Carthage in modern Tunisia was founded by Phoenicians in 814 BCE to ensure commercial domination of the western Mediterranean. The city was soon competing against the region's Greek colonies, some of which became Carthaginian strongholds. Carthage was razed by the Romans in the 2nd century BCE – ruins are all that remain of it today.

fashions; some of Croesus' predecessors had sent offerings to the shrine at Delphi. Now the Hellenization of Lydia went even more quickly ahead. None the less, a much more formidable opponent loomed up even further east: Persia.

GREECE AND PERSIA

THE GREEK STRUGGLE with Persia is the climax of the early history of Greece and the inauguration of the classical age. Because the Greeks made so much of their long conflict with the Persians it is easy to lose sight of the many ties that linked their cultures. The Persian fleets – and to a lesser extent, Persian armies – launched against the Peloponnese had thousands of Greeks, mainly from Ionia, serving in them. Cyrus had employed Greek stone-cutters and sculptors and Darius had a Greek physician. Probably the war did as much to create as to feed the antagonism, however deep the emotional revulsion proclaimed by the Greeks for a country which treated its kings like gods.

The Persian Empire and the Archaemenids

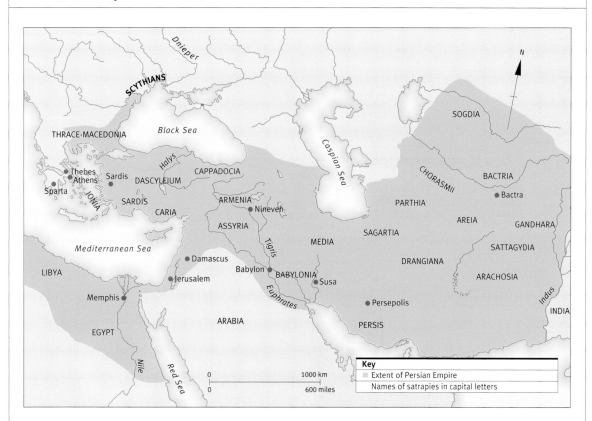

The construction of the great Persian Empire of the Archaemenids began in the middle of the 6th century BCE. In Asia Minor, the Persian king Cyrus the Great defeated the king of Lydia and subjugated the Greek cities on the coast and on a number of Aegean islands. He went on to conquer Babylonia and the lands between the Mediterranean and Mesopotamia. At the end of the 6th century BCE, his son Cambyses conquered Egypt. King Darius continued the empire's expansion to the east, in the Indus valley, and to the west, where he crossed the straits and annexed Thrace and Macedonia in 522–486 BCE. In spite of their greater numbers, however, the Persians were defeated by the Greeks at the battle of Eurymedon in 467 BCE.

THE PERSIAN WAR

The origins of the Persian war lay in the great expansion of Persia under the Achaemenids. In about 540 BCE, the Persians overthrew Lydia (and that was the end of Croesus, who was supposed to have provoked the assault by an incautious interpretation of an utterance of the Delphic oracle, which said that if he went to war with Persia, he would destroy a great empire but not which one). This brought Greeks and Persians face to face; elsewhere, the tide of Persian conquest rolled on. When the Persians took Egypt they damaged Greek traders' interests there. Next, the Persians crossed to Europe and occupied the cities of the coast as far west as Macedon; across the Danube and they failed, and soon retired from Scythia. At this point there was

This amphora dates from the beginning of the 5th century BCE. It illustrates one of the stories about the death of Croesus, king of Lydia, after his capture by the Persian king Cyrus. Croesus is pictured seated on a pyre, about to be burned alive by his captors. This is one of the few pottery decorations from this period whose subject is related to the Persian War.

something of a pause. Then, in the first decade of the fifth century, the Asian Greek cities revolted against Persian suzerainty, encouraged, perhaps, by Darius' failure against the Scythians. The mainland cities, or some of them, decided to help. Athens and Eretria sent a fleet to Ionia. In the subsequent operations the Greeks burnt Sardis, the former capital of Lydia and the seat of the western satrapy of the Persian Empire. But the revolt failed in the end and left the mainland cities facing an enraged opponent.

Things did not usually happen very quickly in the ancient world, and large-scale expeditions still take a long time to prepare, but almost as soon as the Ionian revolt was crushed the Persians sent a fleet against the Greeks; it was wrecked off Mount Athos. A second attempt, in 490 BCE, sacked Eretria but then came to grief at the hands of the Athenians in a battle whose name has become legendary – Marathon.

THE PELOPONNESIAN LEAGUE

Although Marathon was an Athenian victory, the leader in the next phase of the struggle with Persia was Sparta, the strongest of the city-states on land. Out of the Peloponnesian League, an alliance whose origins had been domestic in that its aim had been to assure Sparta's future by protecting her from the need to send her army abroad, there devolved upon Sparta something like national leadership. When the Persians came again, ten years later, almost all the Greek states accepted this – even Athens, whose strengthening of her fleet had made her the preponderant power of the League at sea.

The Greeks said, and no doubt believed, that the Persians came again (in 480 BCE, through Thrace) in millions; if, as now seems more likely, there were in fact well under a

Greek triremes

The navy became increasingly important for Greece's defence during the 5th century BCE. The above bas-relief shows an Athenian trireme – a warship with three rows of oars. This invention has been attributed to the Corinthians, who developed a fleet of warships in the 7th and 6th centuries BCE to protect their merchant navy.

Although the length of a wooden boat could not exceed 125 ft (38 m), because of the risk of the keel being broken out at sea, more oars were needed if speed were to be increased. The trireme solved this problem by using three tiers of rowers, arranged in a way that allowed them sufficient space to operate their oars (see illustration, below). This was also important for the defence of the vessel, as the oars could be retracted quickly when the enemy approached, with the intention of breaking them.

The trireme was a lightweight and highly-manoeuvrable boat. With a well-trained crew of 200 men, the ship could reach a speed of up to 6 miles (10 km) per hour and could easily be steered towards enemy vessels, which it attacked using its large ram.

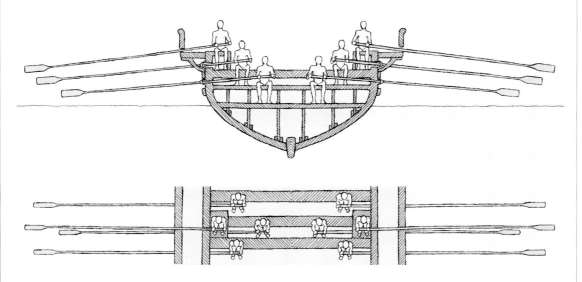

An illustration of a cross-section (above) and bird's-eye view (below) of a Greek trireme.

The Persian War: the battle for the Thermopylae Pass

"As the Persian army advanced to the assault, the Greeks under Leonidas, knowing that they were going to their deaths, went out into the wider part of the pass much further than they had done before; in the previous days' fighting they had been holding the wall and making sorties from behind it into the narrow neck, but now they fought outside the narrows. Many of the invaders fell; behind them the company commanders plied their whips indiscriminately, driving the men on. Many fell into the sea and were drowned, and still more were trampled to death by their friends. No one could count the number of the dead. The Greeks, who knew that the enemy were on their way round by the mountain track and that death was inevitable, put forth all their strength and fought with fury and desperation. By this time most of their spears were broken, and they were killing Persians with their swords.

"In the course of that fight Leonidas fell, having fought most gallantly, and many distinguished Spartans with him – their names I have learned, as those of men who deserve to be remembered..."

An extract from *The Histories* by Herodotus, translated by Aubrey de Sélincourt.

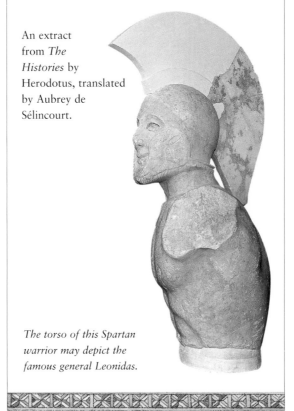

The torso of this Spartan warrior may depict the famous general Leonidas.

This Athenian Greek wine jug dates from the middle of the 5th century BCE. The red-figure painting depicts a fight between a Greek and a Persian soldier – the Greek is shown fighting in the nude, as was the custom, except for a raised Corinthian-style helmet, and is in stark contrast to his Persian enemy, who is bearded and dressed in Asian-style clothes.

hundred thousand of them, this was still an overwhelming enough disproportion for the defenders of Greece. The Persian army moved slowly along the coast and down towards the Peloponnese, accompanied by a huge fleet which hung on its flanks. Yet the Greeks had important advantages in their better-armed and trained heavy infantry, a terrain which nullified the Persian cavalry superiority, and morale.

THE GREEK VICTORY OVER THE PERSIANS

The next crucial battle was at sea. It followed another legendary episode: the overwhelming of Leonidas the Spartan king and his three hundred at the pass of Thermopylae, after which Attica had to be abandoned to the Persians. The Greeks retired to the isthmus of Corinth, their fleet massed in the bay of Salamis near Athens. Time was on their side. It was autumn; a winter which would catch the Persians unprepared would soon be coming and Greek winters are severe. The Persian king threw his numerical advantage away by deciding to engage the Greek fleet in the narrow waters of Salamis. His fleet was shattered and he began a long retreat to the Hellespont. The next year the army he had left behind was defeated at Plataea and the Greeks won another great sea fight, at Mycale on the other side of the Aegean, on the same day. This was the end of the Persian War.

It was a great moment in Greek history, perhaps the greatest, and Sparta and Athens had covered themselves with glory. The liberation of Asiatic Greece followed. It opened an age of huge self-confidence for the Greeks. Their outward drive was to continue until its culmination in a Macedonian empire a century and a half later. The sense of Greek identity was at its height, and people looking back at these heroic days were to wonder

Poseidonia, which was later known as Paestum, was founded in the 8th century BCE in the Bay of Naples. The western façade of the Temple of Poseidon, built in around 450 BCE, is a good example of the simplicity of the Doric style that developed in Magna Graecia. The temple's architect was directly inspired by the Temple of Zeus in Olympia.

later if some great chance to unite Greece as a nation had not then been missed for ever. Perhaps, too, it was something more, for in the repulse of Asia by Greece lay the beginnings of a distinction between Europe and Asia whose reality would not appear for centuries but which would eventually lead people to look back anachronistically at Marathon and Salamis as the first time that Europe was saved.

The red-figure painting on this Attic vase depicts an armed hoplite wearing armour and leg shields and a raised Attic helmet. The vase was found in Caere and dates from c.480 BCE.

3 GREEK CIVILIZATION

Today the Temple of Hephaestus is known as the Theseum, after the images of the hero Theseus that decorate its interior. The temple, which stands on a hill above the Agora of Athens, was converted into a Christian church in the 5th century CE.

VICTORY OVER THE PERSIANS opened the greatest age of Greek history. Some have spoken of a "Greek miracle", so high do the achievements of classical civilization appear. Yet those achievements had as their background a political history so embittered and poisoned that it ended in the extinction of the institution which sheltered Greek civilization, the city-state. Complicated though it is in detail, the story can easily be summarized.

THE DELIAN LEAGUE

For thirty years after the Greek victories at Plataea and Mycale the war with Persia dragged on, but as a background to a more important theme, a sharpening rivalry between Athens and Sparta. Survival assured, the Spartans had gone home with relief, anxious about their helots. This left Athens the undisputed leader of those states which wanted to press ahead with the liberation of other cities from the Persians. A confederation called the Delian League was formed which was to support a common fleet to fight the Persians and command of it was given to an Athenian. As time passed, the members contributed not ships but money. Some did not wish to pay up as the Persian danger declined. Athenian intervention to make sure that they did not default increased and grew harsher. Naxos, for example, which tried to leave the alliance, was besieged back into it. The League was turning gradually into an Athenian empire and the signs were the removal of its headquarters from Delos to Athens, the use of the tribute money for Athenian purposes, the imposition of resident Athenian magistrates and the transfer of important legal cases to Athenian courts. When peace was made with Persia in 449 BCE, the League continued, though its excuse had gone. At its peak, over one hundred and fifty states were paying tribute to Athens.

THE COALITION AGAINST ATHENS

Sparta had welcomed the first stages of the transfer of responsibility to Athens, happy to see others take up commitments outside her own borders. Like other states, Sparta only gradually became aware of a changing situation. When it did, this had much to do with the fact that Athenian hegemony increasingly affected the internal politics of the Greek states. They were often divided about the League, the richer, tax-paying citizens resenting the tribute, while the poorer did not; they did not have to find the money to pay it. When Athenian interventions occurred they were sometimes followed by internal revolution, the result of which was often imitation of Athenian institutions. Athens was herself living through struggles which steadily drove her in the direction of democracy. By 460 BCE, the issue at home was really settled, so that irritation over her diplomatic behaviour soon came to have an ideological flavour. Other things, too, may have added to an irritation with Athens. She was a great trading state and another big trading city, Corinth, felt herself threatened. The Boeotians were directly the subjects of

The Athenian treasury in the sanctuary of Delphi was built to hold valuable offerings to Apollo from the city of Athens. These gifts were intended as a sign of the Athenians' gratitude to the god following their victory over Persia in the battle of Marathon in the year 490 BCE.

This sculpture of a dying warrior is from the sanctuary of Aphaia, Aegina. It dates from the early 5th century BCE and is one of many figures illustrating the deeds of the heroes described in Homer's accounts of the Trojan War.

Athenian aggression, too. The materials thus accumulated for a coalition against Athens, and Sparta eventually took the lead in it by joining in a war against Athens begun in 460. Fifteen years of not very determined fighting followed and then a doubtful peace. It was only after almost another fifteen years, in 431 BCE, that there began the great internal struggle which was to break the back of classical Greece, the Peloponnesian War.

THE PELOPONNESIAN WAR

THE WAR LASTED, with interruptions, twenty-seven years, until 404 BCE. Essentially it was a struggle of land against sea. On one side was the Spartan league, with Boeotia, Macedon (an unreliable ally) and Corinth as Sparta's most important supporters; they held the Peloponnese and a belt of land separating Athens from the rest of Greece. Athens' allies were scattered round the Aegean shore, in the Ionian cities and the islands, the area she had dominated since the days of the Delian League. Strategy was dictated by the means available. Sparta's army, clearly, was best used to occupy Athenian territory and then exact submission. The Athenians could not match their enemies on land. But they had the better navy. This was in large measure the creation of a great Athenian statesman and patriot, the demagogue Pericles. On the fleet he based

The columns of a great Doric temple constructed in about 500 BCE were incorporated into the nave walls of Syracuse cathedral, Sicily, by the builders of the later Christian church.

a strategy of abandoning the Athenian countryside to annual invasion by the Spartans – it was in any case never capable of feeding the population – and withdrawing the inhabitants to the city and its port, the Piraeus, to which it was linked by two walls some five miles long, two hundred yards apart. There the Athenians could sit out the war, untroubled by bombardment or assault, which were beyond the capacities of Greek armies. Their fleet, still controlling the sea, would assure they were fed in war as in peace, by imported corn, so that blockade would not be effective.

Things did not work as well as this, because of plague within the city and the absence of leadership after Pericles' death in 429 BCE, but the basic sterility of the first ten years of the war rests on this strategical deadlock. It brought peace for a time in 421 BCE, but not a lasting one. Athenian frustrations found an outlet in the end in a scheme to carry the war further afield.

THE DEFEAT OF ATHENS

In Sicily lay the rich city of Syracuse, the most important colony of Corinth, herself the greatest of Athens' commercial rivals. To seize Syracuse would deeply wound an

The Peloponnesian War

During the war, the two most powerful Greek city-states, Sparta and Athens, created such complex alliance systems against each other that every state in the Greek world was drawn into the destructive conflict. The war was largely a battle between ground forces and naval forces. Sparta and her allies had solid and well-equipped armies, whereas Athens and the city-states on the Aegean coast had the best fleet. Although the war ended when Athens was forced to capitulate in 404 BCE, there was no true victor – the two states (and their respective allies) had torn each other apart and neither would ever fully recover from the struggle.

Political divisions in the Greek world during the Peloponnesian War.

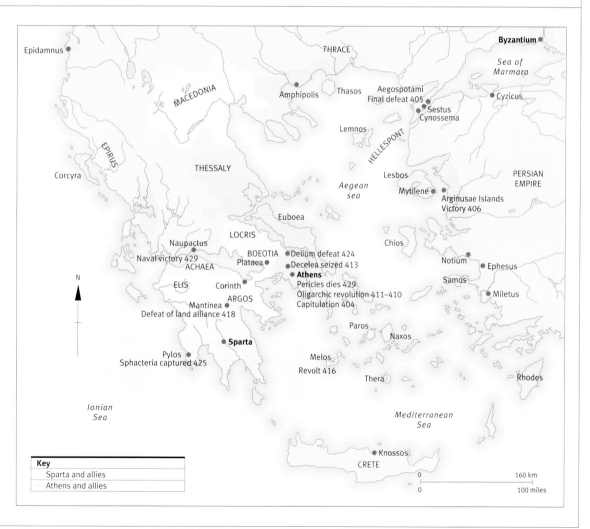

The Athenian historian Thucydides (460–c.400 BCE) fought in the Peloponnesian War and narrated the conflict. His meticulous account of the war constitutes a surprisingly objective historical record. Thucydides persistently sought to expose the causes of events and to explain their outcomes.

enemy, finish off a major grain-supplier to the Peloponnese, and provide immense booty. With this wealth Athens could hope to build and man a yet bigger fleet and thus achieve a final and unquestioned supremacy in the Greek world – perhaps the mastery of the Phoenician city of Carthage and a western Mediterranean hegemony, too. The result was the disastrous Sicilian Expedition of 415–413 BCE. It was decisive, but as a death-blow to the ambitions of Athens. Half her army and all her fleet were lost; a period of political upheaval and disunion began at home. Finally, the defeat crystallized once more the alliance of Athens' enemies.

The Spartans now sought and obtained Persian help in return for a secret undertaking that the Greek cities of mainland Asia should again become vassals of Persia (as they had been before the Persian War). This enabled them to raise the fleet which could help the Athenian subject cities who wanted to shake off her imperial control. Military and naval defeat undermined

morale in Athens. In 411 BCE an unsuccessful revolution replaced the democratic régime briefly with an oligarchy. Then there were more disasters, the capture of the Athenian fleet, and, finally, blockade. This time starvation was effective. In 404 BCE Athens made peace and her fortifications were slighted.

THE CONCLUSION OF THE PELOPONNESIAN WAR

Formally the story ends in 404 BCE, for what followed was implicit in the material and psychological damage the leading states of Greece had done to one another in these bitter years. There followed a brief Spartan hegemony during which she attempted to prevent the Persians cashing the IOU on the Greek Asian cities, but this had to be conceded after a war which brought a revival of Athenian naval power and the rebuilding of the Long Walls. In the end, Sparta and Persia had a common interest in preventing a

Thucydides' *History of the Peloponnesian War*

"In peace and prosperity, states and individuals have better sentiments because they do not find themselves suddenly confronted with imperious necessities; but war takes away the easy supply of daily wants, and so proves a rough master that brings most men's characters to a level with their fortunes. Revolution thus ran its course from city to city, and the places which it arrived at last, from having heard what had been done before, carried to a still greater excess the refinement of their inventions, as manifested in the cunning of their enterprises and the atrocity of their reprisals ... Reckless audacity came to be considered the courage of a loyal ally; prudent hesitation, specious cowardice; moderation was held to be a cloak for unmanliness; ability to see all sides of a question, inaptness to act on any. Frantic violence became the

attribute of manliness; cautious plotting, a justifiable means of self-defence ... Oaths of reconciliation, being only proffered on either side to meet an immediate difficulty, only held good so long as no other weapon was at hand; but when opportunity offered, he who first ventured to seize it and to take his enemy off his guard thought this perfidious vengeance sweeter than an open one, since, considerations of safety apart, success by treachery won him the palm of superior intelligence ... Thus every form of iniquity took root in the Hellenic countries by reason of the troubles ..."

An extract from Book III of the *History of the Peloponnesian War* by Thucydides, translated by Richard Crawley.

renaissance of Athenian power and made peace in 387 BCE. The settlement included a joint guarantee of all the other Greek cities except those of Asia. Ironically, the Spartans soon became as hated as the Athenians had been. Thebes took the leadership of their enemies. At Leuctra, in 371 BCE, to the astonishment of the rest of Greece, the Spartan army was defeated. It marked a psychological and military epoch in something of the same way as the battle of Jena in Prussian history over two thousand years later. The practical consequences made this clear, too; a new confederation was set up in the Peloponnese as a counterweight to Sparta on her very doorstep and the foundation of a revived Messenia in 369 BCE was another blow. The new confederation was a fresh sign that the day of the city-state was passing. The next half-century would see it all but disappear, but 369 BCE is far enough to take the story for the moment.

Such events would be tragic in the history of any country. The passage from the glorious days of the struggle against Persia to the Persians' almost effortless recouping of their losses, thanks to Greek divisions, is a rounded drama which must always grip the imagination. Another reason why such intense interest has been given to it is that it was the subject-matter of an immortal book, Thucydides' *History of the Peloponnesian War*, the first work of contemporary as well as of scientific history. But the fundamental explanation why these few years should fascinate us when greater struggles do not is because we feel that at the heart of the jumble of battles, intrigues, disasters and glory still lies an intriguing and insoluble puzzle: was there a squandering of real opportunities after Mycale, or was this long anticlimax simply a dissipation of an illusion, circumstances having for a moment seemed to promise more than in fact was possible?

This suit of armour, consisting of a bronze Corinthian-style helmet and breastplate, is similar to those that were worn by Greek soldiers during the Peloponnesian War.

FIFTH-CENTURY GREEK CIVILIZATION

THE WAR YEARS have another startling aspect, too. During them there came to fruition the greatest achievement in civilization the world had ever seen. Political and military events then shaped that achievement in certain directions and in the end limited it and determined what should continue to the future. This is why the century or so of this small country's history whose central decades are those of the war is worth as much attention as the millennial empires of antiquity.

At the outset we should recall how small a plinth supported Greek civilization. There were many Greek states, certainly, and they

The minting of coins continued to demonstrate the independence of the *polis*. Some coins, such as the Athenian silver tetradrachma, with its image of Athene and owl symbol, remained practically unchanged from the 6th to the 2nd century BCE.

were scattered over a large expanse of the Aegean, but even if Macedonia and Crete were included, the land-surface of Greece would fit comfortably into England without Wales or Scotland – and of it only about one-fifth could be cultivated. Of the states, most were tiny, containing not more than 20,000 souls at most; the biggest might have had 300,000, thus just surpassing (but not by much) the size of, say, Bournemouth. Within

them only a small élite took part in civic life and the enjoyment of what we now think of as Greek civilization.

The other thing to be clear about at the outset is that civilization's essence. The Greeks were far from underrating comfort and the pleasures of the senses. The physical heritage they left behind set the canons of beauty in many of the arts for two thousand years. Yet in the end the Greeks are remembered as poets and philosophers; it is an achievement of the mind that constitutes their claim on our attention. This has been recognized implicitly in the idea of classical Greece, a creation of later ages rather than of the Greeks themselves. Certainly some Greeks of the fifth and fourth centuries BCE saw themselves as the bearers of a culture which was superior to any other available, but the force of the classical ideal lies in its being a view from a later age, one which looked back to Greece and found there standards by which to assess itself. Later generations saw these standards above all in the fifth century, in the years following victory over the Persians, but there is a certain distortion in this. There is also an Athenian bias in such a view, for the fifth century was the apogee of Athenian cultural success. Nevertheless, to distinguish classical Greece from what went before – usually named "archaic" or "pre-classical" – makes sense. The fifth century has an objective unity because it saw a special heightening

An Attic krater from the first half of the 5th century BCE portraying two great archaic poets from Lesbos, Sappho and Alcaeus. Both became hugely popular in Athens and their poems about love and politics were often recited at gatherings, accompanied by the music of lyres.

This krater depicts a banquet. Apart from the dancers and musicians who entertained the revellers, such festive dinners were attended exclusively by men.

and intensification of Greek civilization, even if that civilization was ineradicably tied to the past, ran on into the future and spilled out over all the Greek world.

ECONOMIC FOUNDATIONS

Greek civilization was rooted still in relatively simple economic patterns; essentially, they were those of the preceding age. No great revolution had altered it since the introduction of money and for three centuries or so there were only gradual or specific changes in the direction or materials of Greek trade. Some markets opened, some closed, but that was all; the technical arrangements grew slightly more elaborate as the years went by. And trade between countries and cities was the most advanced economic sector. Below this level, the Greek economy was still nothing like as complicated as would be now taken for granted. Barter, for example, persisted for everyday purposes well into the era of coinage. It also speaks for relatively simple markets, with only limited demands

made on them by the consumer. The scale of manufacture, too, was small. It has been suggested that at the height of the craze for the best Athenian pottery not more than 150 craftsmen were at work making and painting it. We are not dealing with a world of factories; most craftsmen and traders probably worked as individuals with a few employees and slaves. Even great building projects, such as the embellishment of Athens, reveal subcontracting to small groups of workers. The only exception may have been in mining, where the silver mines of Laurium in Attica seem to have been worked by thousands of slaves, though the arrangements under which this was done – the mines belonged to the state and were in some way sublet – remain obscure. The heart of the economy almost everywhere was subsistence agriculture. In spite of the specialized demand and production of an Athens or a Miletus (which had something of a name as a producer of woollens) the typical community depended on the production by small farmers of the grain, olives, vines and timber needed by the home market.

A black-figure Corinthian plaque dating from the beginning of the 6th century BCE. Baked-clay plaques such as this one were offered as *ex votos*: some showed gods, others portrayed simple work scenes. Here, clay is being extracted from a pit. This was the first stage in the production of pottery – a vitally important commodity for Corinthian trade.

The decoration on this 5th-century BCE ceramic depicts preparations for a nuptial ceremony. The seated young woman is waiting for a slave to put her necklace on.

GREEK MEN

Men who worked small farms were the typical Greeks. Some were rich, most of them were probably poor by modern standards, but even now the Mediterranean climate makes a relatively low income more tolerable than it would be elsewhere. Commerce on any scale, and other kinds of entrepreneurial activity, were likely to be mainly in the hands of metics. They might have considerable social standing and were often rich men, but (for example) in Athens they could not acquire land without special permission, though they were liable for military service (which gives us a little information about their numbers, for at the beginning of the Peloponnesian War there were some 3000 who could afford the arms and armour needed to serve as hoplite infantry). The other male inhabitants of the city-state who were not citizens were either freemen or slaves.

GREEK WOMEN

Women, too, were excluded from citizenship, though it is hazardous to generalize any further about their legal rights. In Athens, for example, they could neither inherit nor own property, though both were possible in Sparta, nor could they undertake a business transaction if more than the value of a bushel of grain was involved. Divorce at the suit of the wife was, it is true, available to Athenian women, but it seems to have been rare and was probably practically harder to obtain

Euripides' *Trojan Women*

"All the accomplishments that bring credit to a woman I strove to put into practice in the house of Hector. In the first instance, in the matter where a woman gets a bad reputation (whether she attracts criticism or not), namely, not remaining indoors, I suppressed my longing and stayed in the house. And inside the home I would not tolerate the idle gossip of women but was content to have in my own mind a teacher I could trust. I kept a quiet tongue in my husband's presence and let no clouds pass over my face. I knew in which matters I should be superior to my husband and when it was right for me to let him prevail. And it was because my reputation for this reached the ears of the Greek army that my doom was sealed. For once I was a captive, Achilles' son wished to take me as his wife. I shall be a slave in a murderer's house.

"Now if I dismiss any thought of my beloved Hector and open my heart to my new husband, it will seem that I have betrayed the dead ..."

An extract from Andromache's speech from *Trojan Women* by Euripides, translated by John Davie.

than it was for men, who seem to have been able to get rid of wives fairly easily. Literary evidence suggests that wives other than those of rich men lived, for the most part, the lives of drudges. The social assumptions that governed all women's behaviour were very restrictive; even women of the upper classes stayed at home in seclusion for most of the time. If they ventured out, they had to be accompanied; to be seen at a banquet put their respectability in question. Entertainers and courtesans were the only women who could normally expect a public life; they could enjoy a certain celebrity, but a respectable woman could not. Significantly, in classical Greece girls were thought unworthy of education. Such attitudes suggest the primitive atmosphere of the society out of which they grew, one very different from, say, Minoan Crete among its predecessors, or later Rome.

SEXUALITY

So far as sexuality is revealed by literature, Greek marriage and parenthood could produce deep feeling and as high a mutual regard between individual men and women as in our own societies. One element in it which is nowadays hard to weigh up exactly was a tolerated and even romanticized male homosexuality. Convention regulated this. In many Greek cities, it was acceptable for young upper-class males to have love-affairs with older men (interestingly, there is much less evidence in Greek literature of homosexual love between men of the same age). This was not thought to disqualify them for subsequent heterosexual marriage. Something must be allowed for fashion in this, but all societies can provide examples of homosexual relationships which suit many men at one stage of their lives; those of the ancient

This *kore* (a statue of a woman), dates from the beginning of the 5th century BCE and marks the move from the archaic style to classicism. *Korai* statues, many of which bear traces of polychromatism, were usually placed in sanctuaries as offerings to the gods. Male *kouroi* figures were often made as grave-markers.

Athenian education

Until they were six or seven years old, Athenian children lived at home in separate apartments inhabited exclusively by women and other children. The boys then attended school, while girls remained secluded in the house and were not given a formal education. Sons of wealthy citizens were accompanied to school by a slave, who was known as the "pedagogue".

Teachers were independent and charged parents directly for their services; they taught pupils how to read, write and count and had them learn verses by Homer and Hesiod by rote. Music lessons were also important, as were gymnastics classes, which took place in the *palestras*, where the boys were taught the main athletic exercises.

At the age of 15, youths began to attend gymnasiums where they frequented discussions with philosophers and practised athletics in preparation for military service. After the two-year course that constituted an *ephebe*, young men began their military training, often continuing to visit the gymnasium.

An illustration entitled "The poet Linos tutoring the young Mousaios" from a 5th-century BCE dish.

Greeks have attracted undue attention, perhaps because of the absence of inhibitions and controls which made the expression of homosexual affection improper in other societies and because the general prestige of their civilization has rubbed off on even its minor embodiments. At root, it may only have been a function of the restrictions which segregated and circumscribed the lives of free women.

GREEK SOCIETY

In sexual matters as in everything else we know much more about the behaviour of an élite than about that of most Greeks. Citizenship, which must often have spanned very different social levels in practice, is a category too big to permit generalizations. Even in democratic Athens the kind of man who rose in public life and of whom, therefore, we read in the records, was usually a landowner; he was not likely to be a businessman, far less a craftsman. A craftsman might be important as a member of his group in the assembly, but he could hardly make his way to leadership. Businessmen may have been handicapped by the long-engrained conviction of upper-class Greeks that trade and industry were no proper occupations for a gentleman, who should ideally live a life of cultivated leisure based on the revenues of his own lands. This was a view which was to pass into European tradition with important effect.

Social history therefore blurs into politics. The Greek preoccupation with political life – the life of the *polis* – and the fact that classical Greece is neatly delimited by two distinct political epochs (that of the Persian Wars and that of a new, Macedonian, empire) makes it easy to appreciate the importance of Greek

A parade of riders from one of the friezes that decorated the Parthenon of Athens. These young men, depicted taking part in a procession in honour of Athene, represented the vitality of the Athenian élite. It is likely that they commemorated the young men killed fighting for Athens and Greece against Persia at Marathon.

political history to civilization. Yet to reconstruct it in any complete sense is impossible. Many, perhaps most, English parishes have records richer than those we can recover for most of the city-states of Greece. What can be discovered from the evidence is much of the history of Athens, quite a lot of that of a few other states, almost nothing of many, and a fairly full narrative of their relations with one another. Together, these facts provide us with a pretty clear picture of the political context of classical Greek civilization, but uncertainty about many of its details.

Athens dangerously dominates this picture. There are big risks in arguing too readily from Athens to what was typical. What we know most about we often tend to think most important and because some of the greatest of fifth-century Greeks were Athenians and Athens is one pole of the great story of the Peloponnesian War, scholars have

given its history enormous attention. Yet we also know that Athens was – to take only two points – both big and a commercial centre; it must, therefore, have been very untypical in important ways.

ATHENIAN PRIMACY

THE TEMPTATION TO OVER-VALUE Athens' cultural importance is less dangerous. Such a primacy was, after all, recognized at the time. Though many of the greatest Greeks were not Athenians, and many Greeks rejected the Athenians' claims to superiority, the Athenians felt themselves the leaders of Greece. Only a few of the most scrupulous among them hesitated to use the tribute of the Delian League for embellishing its leading city. Thus were built the buildings whose ruins still crown the Acropolis, the

The Acropolis of Athens

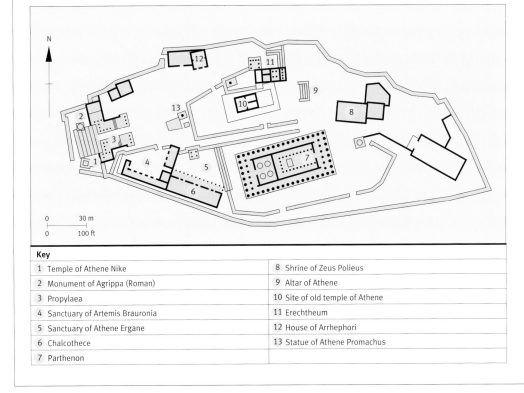

Key	
1 Temple of Athene Nike	8 Shrine of Zeus Polieus
2 Monument of Agrippa (Roman)	9 Altar of Athene
3 Propylaea	10 Site of old temple of Athene
4 Sanctuary of Artemis Brauronia	11 Erechtheum
5 Sanctuary of Athene Ergane	12 House of Arrhephori
6 Chalcothece	13 Statue of Athene Promachus
7 Parthenon	

Athens' Acropolis crowned a steep-sided, easily defensible rock, upon which various ancient buildings had once stood, including a Bronze Age Mycenaean palace. During the Classical Age, the city's main religious sanctuaries and temples were located at the site. The Acropolis was reduced to ruins during the war with Persia in the first half of the 5th century BCE. After the end of the war, the Athenian general and statesman Pericles oversaw an extensive rebuilding programme and initiated the construction of several magnificent monuments and temples, some of which were completed after his death in 429 BCE. The Romans later added to the complex.

A plan showing the main buildings in the Athenian Acropolis.

A view of the western façade of the Ionic-style temple on the Acropolis at Athens known as the Erechtheum (it originally housed the tomb of the hero Erechtheus). Building work on the temple began in 421 BCE. The olive tree in the foreground is the sacred tree of the goddess Athene, patroness of the city. On the southern façade is the famous porch of six caryatids (statues of female figures used as columns).

Parthenon and Propylaea, but, of course, the money spent on them was available just because so many Greek states recognized Athens' paramountcy. This reality is what the tribute lists record. When on the eve of the Peloponnesian War Pericles told his countrymen that their state was a model for the rest of Greece there was an element of propaganda in what he said, but there was also conviction.

GEOGRAPHICAL ADVANTAGES

Solid grounds for the importance traditionally given to Athens ought, indeed, to be suggested *a priori* by the basic facts of geography. Her position recalls the tradition that she played an ill-defined but seemingly important role in the Ionian plantation of the Aegean and Asia Minor. Easy access to this region, together with poor agricultural resources, made her a trading and maritime power early in the sixth century. Thanks to this she was the richest of the Greek cities;

at the end of it the discovery of the silver deposits of Laurium gave her the windfall with which to build the fleet of Salamis. From the fleet came her undisputed pre-eminence in the Aegean and thence, eventually, the tribute which refreshed her treasury in the fifth century. The peak of her power and wealth was reached just before the Peloponnesian War, in the years when creative activity and patriotic inspiration reached their height. Pride in the extension of empire was then linked to a cultural achievement which was truly enjoyed by the people.

THE ATHENIAN NAVY

Commerce, the navy, ideological confidence and democracy are themes as inseparably and traditionally interwoven in the history of fifth-century Athens as of late nineteenth-century England, though in very different ways. It was widely recognized at the time that a fleet of ships whose movement depended ultimately upon about two hundred paid oarsmen apiece was both the instrument of imperial power and the preserve of the democracy. Hoplites were less important in a naval state than elsewhere, and no expensive armour was needed to be an oarsman, who would be paid by the tribute of the League or the proceeds of successful warfare – as it was hoped, for example, the Sicilian Expedition would prove. Imperialism was genuinely popular among Athenians who would expect to share its profits, even if only indirectly and collectively, and not to have to bear its burdens. This was an aspect of Athenian democracy which was given much attention by its critics.

ATHENIAN DEMOCRACY

ATTACKS ON ATHENIAN DEMOCRACY began in early times and have continued ever since. They have embodied as much historical misrepresentation as have over-zealous

and idealizing defences of the same institutions. The misgivings of frightened conservatives who had never seen anything like it before are understandable, for democracy emerged at Athens unexpectedly and at first almost unobserved. Its roots lay in sixth-century constitutional changes which replaced the organizing principle of kinship with that of locality; in theory and law, at least, local attachment came to be more important than the family you belonged to. This was a development which appears to have been general in Greece and it put democracy on the localized institutional basis

This red-figure Attic cup was painted by Brygos at the beginning of the 5th century BCE and depicts an Athenian democratic voting session. Athene presides over the scene, wearing her emblematic helmet and surrounded by citizens who are about to vote.

Basic institutions and democracy at work in Athens

ECCLESIA: An assembly composed of all Athenian citizens, which met at least 40 times per year. Only those who were 18 years old or over, male, free and of Athenian parents could be citizens, which meant that a large portion of the population was excluded from public life. The ecclesia took decisions concerning important affairs – decrees were voted on following a public discussion.

BOULE: A council formed by 500 citizens, all over 30 years old and generally with public experience, chosen by a draw. The boule prepared the work to be carried out by the ecclesia, studying the drafts for laws. It also controlled foreign policy and the administration of the city. The boule was divided into ten sections, called prytaneas, which rotated during the year. The acting councillors were called prytaneans.

MAGISTRATES: Magistrates wielded considerable power. Candidates underwent a detailed interrogation by the boule about their morality. Most posts were assigned by a draw. The magistrates' work consisted of guaranteeing the administration of the various public services and making sure that the decisions taken by the ecclesia and the boule were carried out. Among the elected magistrates, the strategists were extremely powerful because they were heads of the army and the navy and intervened in matters concerning war and peace. Although magistrates could only stay in office for one year, there was no limit to the number of times they could be re-elected and, if they had exceptional administrative abilities or oratory skills, individuals were often able to prolong their term of office. The famous general Pericles, for example, served as a magistrate for 30 years.

DIKASTERIA: A popular tribune formed by 6,000 jurists. The jurists were assigned annually by a draw from candidates who were more than 30 years old.

These pieces of pottery are *ostrakas*, on which voters wrote the name of a citizen to be ostracized (exiled from Athens) for 10 years. Intended to restrict the power of individuals in 5th-century BCE Athens, ostracism could be misused – it became evident that intrigue limited its effectiveness.

which it has usually had ever since. Other changes followed from this. By the middle of the fifth century all adult males were entitled to take part in the assembly and through it, therefore, in the election of major administrative officers. The powers of the Areopagus were steadily reduced; after 462 BCE it was only a law-court with jurisdiction over certain offences. The other courts were at the same time rendered more susceptible to democratic influence by the institution of payment for jury-service. As they also conducted much administrative business, this meant a fair amount of popular participation in the daily running of the city. Just after the Peloponnesian War, when times were hard, pay was also offered for attendance at the assembly itself. Finally, there was the Athenian belief in selecting by lot; its use for the choice of magistrates told against hereditary prestige and power.

POLITICIANS

At the root of the Athenian constitution lay distrust of expertise and entrenched authority and confidence in collective common sense. From this derived, no doubt, the relative lack of interest Athenians showed in rigorous jurisprudence – argument in an Athenian court was occupied much more with questions of motive, standing and substance, than with questions of law – and the importance they gave to the skills of oratory. The effective political leaders of Athens were those who could sway their fellow-citizens by their words. Whether we call them demagogues or orators does not matter; they were the first politicians seeking power by persuasion.

Towards the end of the fifth century, though even then by no means usually, some such men came from families outside the traditional ruling class. The continuing importance of old political families was nevertheless an important qualification of the democratic system. Themistocles at the beginning of the century and Pericles when the war began were members of old families, their birth making it proper for them even in the eyes of conservatives to take the lead in affairs; the old ruling classes found it easier to accept democracy because of this practical qualification of it. There is a rough parallel in the grudging acceptance of Whig reform by nineteenth-century English aristocrats; government in Athens as in Victorian England remained for a long time in the hands of men whose forefathers might have expected to rule the state in more aristocratic days. Another tempering qualification was provided by the demands of politics on time and money. Though jurors and members of the assembly might be paid, the fee for attendance was small; it seems to have been prompted, too, by the need to make sure of a quorum, which does not suggest that the assembly found it easy to get the mass of the citizens to attend. Many of them must have lived too far away and it has been

FOREIGN POLICY

Even in its emergent period Athenian democracy was identified with adventure and enterprise in foreign policy. Popular demand lay behind support for the Greek cities of Asia in their revolt against Persia. Later, for understandable reasons, it gave foreign policy an anti-Spartan bias. The struggle against the Areopagus was led by Themistocles, the builder of the Athenian fleet of Salamis, who had sensed a potential danger from Sparta from the moment the Persian War was over. Thus the responsibility for the Peloponnesian War and for its exacerbation of the factions and divisions of all the other cities of Greece came to be laid at the door of democracy. It not only brought disaster upon Athens itself, its critics pointed out, but exported to or at least awoke in all the Greek cities the bitterness of faction and social conflict. Oligarchy was twice restored in Athens – not that it helped matters – and by the end of the century faith in Athenian decmocracy was grievously weakened. Thucydides could take his history only down to 411 BCE but it closes in misgiving and disillusion over his native city – which had exiled him – and Plato was to imprint for ever upon the Athenian democrats the stigma of the execution of Socrates in 399 BCE.

The Athenian politician Pericles was a decisive force in democratic Athenian politics for 30 years. This bust of Pericles is a Roman copy of an original by Cresilas made at the end of the 5th century BCE. The helmet alludes to Pericles' strategic skills and his regular features recall the idealized portrayal of classical figures.

calculated that not more than about one in eight of them were present at the usual statutory meetings, of which some forty were held each year. These facts tend to be lost to sight both in the denunciation and the idealization of Athenian democracy and they go some way to explaining its apparent mildness. Taxation was light and there was little discriminatory legislation against the rich such as we would now associate with democratic rule and such as Aristotle said would be the inevitable result of the rule of the poor.

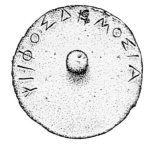
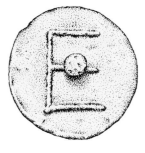

To cast their votes, the Athenians used small bronze pieces or clay tablets such as these. The tiny handles on each piece were hollow or solid, depending on whether the vote was for an acquittal or a conviction.

THE ACHIEVEMENTS OF ATHENIAN DEMOCRACY

If Athenian democracy's exclusion of women, metics and slaves is also placed in the scale, the balance against it seems heavy; to modern eyes, it looks both narrow and disastrously unsuccessful. Yet it should not disqualify Athens for the place she later won in the regard of posterity. Anachronistic and invalid comparisons are too easy; Athens is not to be compared with ideals still imperfectly realized after two thousand years, but with her contemporaries. For all the survival of the influence of the leading families and the practical impossibility that even a majority of its members would turn up to any particular meeting of the assembly, more Athenians were engaged in self-government than was the case in any other state. Athenian democracy more than any other institution brought about the liberation of men from the political ties of kin which is one of the great Greek achievements. Many who could not have contemplated office elsewhere could experience in Athens the political education of taking responsible decisions which is the heart of political culture. Men of modest means could help to run the institutions which nurtured and protected Athens' great civilized achievement. They listened to arguments of an elevation and thoughtfulness which makes it impossible to dismiss them as mere rhetoric; they must surely have weighed them seriously *sometimes*. Just as the physical divisions between the old Greek communities fostered a variety of experience which led in the end to a break with the world of god-given rulers and a grasp of the idea that political arrangements could be consciously chosen, so the stimulus of participation in affairs worked on unprecedentedly large numbers of men in classical Athens, not only in the assembly, but in the daily meetings of the people's council which prepared its business. Even without the eligibility of all citizens to office Athenian democracy would still have been the greatest instrument of political education contrived down to that time.

It is against that background that the errors, vanities and misjudgments of Athenian politics must be seen. We do not cease to treasure the great achievements of British political culture because of the shallowness and corruptness of much of twentieth-century democracy. Athens may be judged, like any political system, by its working at its best; under the leadership of Pericles it was outstanding. It left behind the myth of the individual's responsibility for his own political fate. We need myths in politics and have yet to find a better.

THE CONCEPT OF "VIRTUE"

The Athenians, in any case, would have been uninterested in many modern

A fragment of the Parthenon's east frieze, sculpted in 442–432 BCE, depicting Hephaestus, Apollo and Artemis. This group of divinities is one of those which, together with the frieze on the Parthenon's main façade, greeted the long procession of the Panathenaea, in which the whole city of Athens took part.

criticisms of their democracy. Its later defenders and attackers have both often fallen into another sort of anachronism, that of misinterpreting the goals Greeks thought worth achieving. Greek democracy, for example, was far from being dominated, as is ours, by the mythology of cooperativeness, and cheerfully paid a larger price in destructiveness than would be welcomed today. There was a blatant competitiveness in Greek life apparent from the Homeric poems onwards. Greeks admired men who won and thought men should strive to win. The consequent release of human power was colossal, but also dangerous. The ideal expressed in the much-used word which we inadequately translate as "virtue" illustrates this. When Greeks used it, they meant that people were able, strong, quick-witted, just as much as just, principled, or virtuous in a modern sense. Homer's hero, Odysseus, frequently behaved like a rogue, but he is brave and clever and he succeeds; he is therefore admirable. To show such quality was good; it did not matter that the social cost might sometimes be high. The Greek was concerned with "face"; his culture taught him to avoid shame rather than guilt and the fear of shame was never far from the fear of public evidence of guilt. Some of the explanation of the bitterness of faction in Greek politics lies here; it was a price willingly paid.

When all is said, Athenian democracy must be respected above all for what it cradled, a series of cultural triumphs which are peaks even in the history of Greek civilization. These were public facts. The art of Athens was applauded and sustained by many people; the tragedies were tested not by the takings of a box-office but by

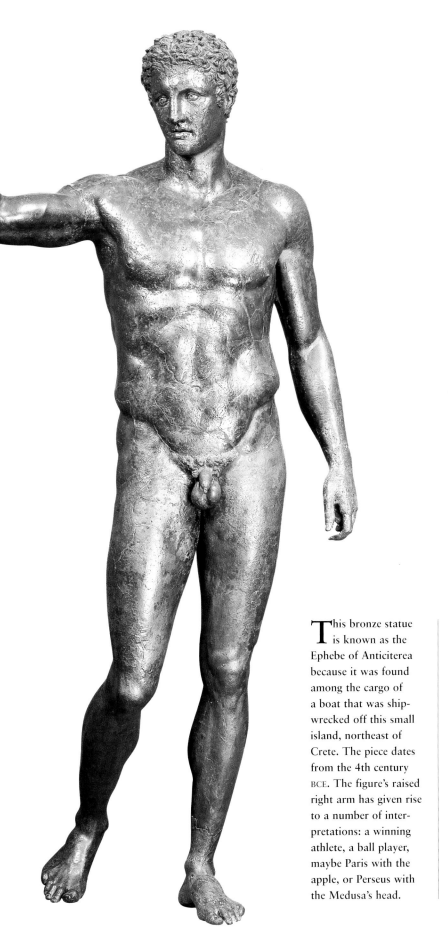

This bronze statue is known as the Ephebe of Anticiterea because it was found among the cargo of a boat that was shipwrecked off this small island, northeast of Crete. The piece dates from the 4th century BCE. The figure's raised right arm has given rise to a number of interpretations: a winning athlete, a ball player, maybe Paris with the apple, or Perseus with the Medusa's head.

judges interpreting a public taste vigorously expressed. The sculptor Phidias worked to beautify the city and not for an individual patron. And as democracy degenerated, so it seems, there was a waning of artistic nerve. This was a loss to the whole of Greece.

PHILOSOPHICAL QUESTIONING

The achievement which made Greece teacher of Europe (and through her of the world) is too rich and varied to generalize about even in long and close study; it is impossible to summarize in a page or so. But there is a salient theme which emerges in it: a growing confidence in rational, conscious enquiry. If civilization is advance towards the control of mentality and environment by reason, then the Greeks did more for it than any of their predecessors. They invented the philosophical question as part and parcel of one of the great intuitions of all time, that a coherent and logical explanation of things could be found, that the world did not ultimately rest upon the meaningless and arbitrary fiat of gods or demons. Put like that, of course, it is not an attitude which could be or was grasped by all, or even most, Greeks. It was an attitude which had to make its way in a world permeated with irrationality and superstition. Nevertheless, it was a revolutionary and beneficial idea. It looked forward to the possibility of a society where such an attitude would be generalized; even Plato, who thought it impossible that most people could share it, gave to the rulers of his ideal state the task of rational reflexion as the justification both of their privileges and of the discipline laid upon them. The Greek challenge to the weight of irrationality

The work of the dramatic poet Aeschylus (525–456 BCE), including the famous Oresteia Trilogy, explored his belief that humanity's destiny was decided by supernatural forces.

in social and intellectual activity tempered its force as it had never been tempered before. For all the subsequent exaggeration and myth-making about it, the liberating effect of this emphasis was felt again and again for thousands of years. It was the greatest single Greek achievement.

POPULAR SUPERSTITION

The enormity of the revolution in modes of thought in the Aegean means that it now obscures its own scale. So remarkable are the works of the Greek intellectuals and so large have they loomed that it requires effort to penetrate through them to the values of the world from which they emerged. It is made a little easier because no such revolution is ever complete. A look at the other side of the coin reveals that most Greeks continued to live in cocoons of traditional irrationality and superstition; even those who were in a position to understand something of the speculations which were opening new mental worlds rarely accepted the implications. A continuing respect was shown to the old public orthodoxies. It was impiety in late fifth-century Athens, for example, to deny belief in the gods. One philosopher believed that the sun was a red-hot disc; it did not protect him that he had been the friend of Pericles when he said so, and he had to flee. It was at Athens, too, that public opinion was convulsed, on the eve of the Sicilian Expedition, by the mysterious and ominous mutilation of certain public statues, the "Hermae", or busts of Hermes. The disasters which followed were attributed by some to this sacrilege. Socrates, the Athenian philosopher who became, thanks to his pupil

Plato, the archetypal figure of the man of intellect, and left as a maxim the view that "the unexamined life is not worth living", offended the pieties of his state and was condemned to die for it by his fellow-citizens; he was also condemned for questioning received astronomy. It does not seem that similar trials took place elsewhere, but they imply a background of popular superstition which must have been more typical of the Greek community than the presence of a Socrates.

GREEK THOUGHT

In spite of important historical residues, Greek thought, more than that of any earlier civilization, reflected changes of emphasis and fashion. They arose from its own dynamism and did not always lead to a greater ability to grapple with nature and society rather than surrender to them, but sometimes to dead ends and blind alleys, to exotic and extravagant fantasies. Greek thought is not monolithic; we should think not of a bloc with a unity pervading all its parts, but of a historical continuum extending across three or four centuries, in which different elements are prominent at different times and which is hard to assess.

One reason for this is that Greek categories of thought – the way, so to speak, in which they laid out the intellectual map before beginning to think about its individual components in detail at all – are not our own, though often deceptively like them. Some of those we use did not exist for the Greeks and their knowledge led them to draw different boundaries between fields of enquiry from those which we take for granted. Sometimes this is obvious and presents no difficulties; when a philosopher, for example, locates the

The ruins of the temple of Apollo and its foundations in the sanctuary at Delphi. The temple's altar was situated in front of these restored columns. The details of the inner design, where the famous oracle of the god Apollo was consulted, can still be discerned.

Miletus

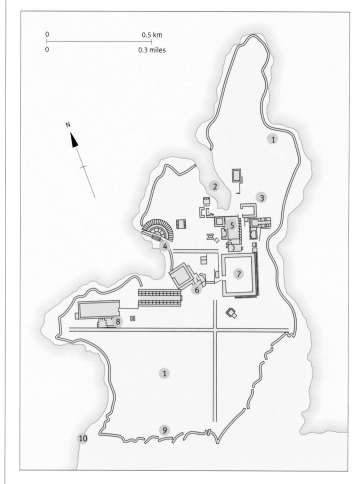

Key	
1	Residential quarters
2	Lion Bay
3	Delphinium
4	Theatre
5	North Agora
6	Baths
7	South Agora
8	Temple of Athene
9	City walls
10	Ancient coastline

Located at the mouth of the Maeander River on the Aegean coast, Miletus was once the most important Greek city in Asia. Its remains also testify to the fact that it was a major centre of philosophical and scientific thought in the 6th century BCE.

A plan of the classical city of Miletus.

Today the theatre at Miletus, built in the Hellenistic period and altered on many occasions, preserves the appearance that it was given by the Romans. It was the largest theatre in Asia and could seat 15,000 spectators.

A Roman bust of the philosopher Socrates, who was born in 470 BCE in Athens. Socrates' teachings are known to us through the work of his disciple Plato.

The Great Gate of the south Agora of Miletus, of which this is a detail, was built in the 1st century CE. This is a good example of Hellenistic architecture – the monumental façade is organized independently from the structure and floor plan of the building.

management of the household and its estate (economics) as a part of a study of what we should call politics, we are not likely to misunderstand him. In more abstract topics it can cause trouble.

GREEK SCIENCE

FOR US, SCIENCE SEEMS TO BE an appropriate way of approaching the understanding of the physical universe, and its techniques are those of empirical experiment and observation. Greek thinkers found the nature of the physical universe just as approachable through abstract thought, through metaphysics, logic and mathematics. It has been said that Greek rationality actually came in the end to stand in the way of scientific progress, because enquiry followed logic and

abstract deduction, rather than the observation of nature. Among the great Greek philosophers, only Aristotle gave prominence to collecting and classifying data, and he did this for the most part only in his social and biological studies. This is one reason for not separating the history of Greek science and philosophy too violently. They are a whole, the product of scores of cities and developing across four centuries or so in time.

THE MILETAN SCHOOL

The beginnings of Greek science and philosophy constitute a revolution in human thought and it has already taken place when there appear the earliest Greek thinkers of whom we have information. They lived in the Ionian city of Miletus in the seventh and sixth centuries BCE. Important intellectual activity went on there and in other Ionian cities right down to the remarkable age of Athenian speculation which begins with Socrates. No doubt the stimulus of an Asian background was important here as in so

A view of the ruins of Miletus, in present-day Turkey. In the background stands the Nymphaion, which dates from the 2nd century CE. In the foreground lie the remains of Corinthian capitals, decorated with acanthus leaves.

many other ways in getting things started; it may also have been significant that Miletus was a rich place; early thinkers seem to have been rich men who could afford the time to think. None the less, the early emphasis on Ionia gives way before long to a spectrum of intellectual activity going on all over the Greek world. The western settlements of Magna Graecia and Sicily were crucial in many sixth- and fifth-century developments and primacy in the later Hellenistic age was to go to Alexandria. The whole Greek world was involved in the success of the Greek mind and even the great age of Athenian questioning should not be given exaggerated standing within it.

In the sixth century BCE Thales and Anaximander launched at Miletus the conscious speculation about the nature of the universe which shows that the crucial boundary between myth and science has been crossed. Egyptians had set about the practical manipulation of nature and had learned much inductively in the process, while Babylonians had made important measurements. The Miletan school made good use of this information, and possibly took more fundamental cosmological notions from the old civilizations, too; Thales is said to have held that the earth had its origin in water. Yet the Ionian philosophers soon went beyond their inheritance. They set out a general view of the nature of the universe which replaced myth with impersonal explanation. This is more impressive than the fact that the specific answers they put forward were in the end to prove unfruitful. The Greek analysis of the nature of matter is an example. Although an atomic theory was adumbrated which was over two thousand years before its time, this was by the fourth century rejected in favour of a view, based on that of the early Ionian thinkers, that all matter was composed of four "elements" – air, water, earth, fire – which combined in different proportions in different substances. This theory subsequently dominated western science down to the Renaissance. It was of enormous historical importance because of the boundaries it set and the possibilities it opened. It was also, of course, erroneous.

LEGACY OF IONIAN TRADITION

The fear that the theory of the elements was wrong should be firmly kept in place as a secondary consideration at this point. What mattered about the Ionians and the school they founded was what has rightly been called their "astonishing" novelty. They pushed aside gods and demons from the understanding of nature. Time was to overwhelm some of what they had done, it is true. In Athens in the late fifth century more than a temporary alarm in the face of defeat and danger has been seen in the condemnation as blasphemous of views far less daring than those of Ionian thinkers two centuries before. One of them had said "If the ox could paint a picture, his god would look like an ox"; a few centuries later, classical Mediterranean civilization has lost much of such perceptiveness. Its early appearance is the most striking sign of the vigour of Greek civilization.

Not only popular superstition swamped such ideas. Other philosophical tendencies also played a part. One coexisted with the Ionian tradition for a long time and was to have much longer life and influence. Its crux

was the view that reality was immaterial, that, as Plato later put it in one of its most persuasive expressions, in life we experience only the images of pure Form and Ideas, the heavenly embodiments of true reality, which can only be apprehended by thought, a matter not only of systematic speculation, but of intuition, too. For all its immateriality, this kind of thinking also had its roots in Greek science, though not in the speculations of the Ionians about matter but in the activities of mathematicians.

MATHEMATICS

Some of the Greek mathematicians' greatest advances were not to be made until long after Plato's death, when they would round off what is the biggest single triumph of Greek thought, its establishment of most of the arithmetic and geometry which served western civilization down to the seventeenth century. Every schoolboy used to know the name of Pythagoras, who lived at Crotone in southern Italy in the middle of the sixth century and may be said to have founded the deductive proof. Fortunately or unfortunately, he did more than this. He discovered the mathematical basis of harmonics by studying a vibrating string and he became especially interested in the relationship of numbers and geometry. His approach to them was semi-mystical; Pythagoras, like many mathematicians, was a religiously minded man who is said to have celebrated the satisfactory conclusion of his famous proof by sacrificing an ox. His school – there was a secret Pythagorean "Brotherhood" – later came to hold that the ultimate nature of the universe was mathematical and numerical. "They fancied that the principles of mathematics were the principles of all things," reported Aristotle, somewhat

The philosopher Pythagoras was born in the 6th century BCE in Samos. He later settled in the Sicilian city of Crotone, where he founded a philosophical school that operated in a similar way to a religious sect.

Hippocrates

Hippocrates was born into a family of doctors on the island of Cos in around 460 BCE. At a time when the treatment of illnesses was mainly governed by superstition, Hippocrates claimed that medicine was a science that should be taught and discussed openly. The teachers from the medical school he established at Cos published a large number of texts, of which around 70 have survived, under the name of Hippocrates. Although none of the published works are believed actually to have been written by Hippocrates, their contents are clearly influenced by his scientific research and teaching. Topics covered include women and children's illnesses, dietary and drug treatments, surgery and medical ethics. Although the texts attributed to him have now been scientifically surpassed, the work of Hippocrates still contains a lucid analysis of contemporary medicine and medical practice.

A detail from the Roman fresco "Galenus and Hippocrates" from the crypt of a church in Anagni, Latium, depicting Hippocrates – the "father of medicine".

disapprovingly, yet his own teacher, Plato, had been greatly influenced by this belief, and by the scepticism of Parmenides, an early fifth-century Pythagorean, about the world known to the senses. Numbers seemed more attractive than the physical world; they possessed both the defined perfection and the abstraction of the Idea which embodied reality.

ASTRONOMY

Pythagorean influence on Greek thought is an immense subject; fortunately, it need not be summarized. What matters here is its ultimate repercussions in a view of the universe which, because it was constructed on mathematical and deductive principles, rather than from observation, fixed astronomy on the wrong lines for nearly two thousand years. From it came the vision of a universe built up of successively enclosing spheres on which moved sun, moon and planets in a fixed and circular pattern about the earth. The Greeks noticed that this did not seem to be the way the heavens moved in practice. But, to summarize crudely, appearances were saved by introducing more and more refinements into the basic scheme while refusing to scrutinize the principles from which it was deduced. The final elaborations were not achieved until work in the second century CE by a famous Alexandrian, Ptolemy. These efforts were remarkably successful, and only a few dissentients demurred (which shows that other intellectual results were possible in Greek science). For all the inadequacies of Ptolemy's system, predictions of planetary movement could be made which would still serve as adequate guides for oceanic navigation in the age of Columbus, even if they rested on misconceptions which sterilized cosmological thinking until his day.

Both the theory of the four elements and

List of the major Greek philosophers

Pre-Socratic
Thales of Miletus (6th century BCE, first half)
Anaximander of Miletus (6th century BCE, first half)
Anaximenes of Miletus (6th century BCE, second half)
Xenophanes of Colophon (6th century BCE, second half)
Pythagoras of Samos (6th century BCE, second half)
Parmenides of Elea (5th century BCE, first half)
Heraclitus of Ephesus (5th century BCE, first half)
Empedocles of Acragas (5th century BCE, middle)
Anaxagoras of Clazomenae (5th century BCE, middle)
Leucippus (5th century BCE, middle)
Democritus (5th century BCE, middle)
Zeno of Elea (5th century BCE, middle)
Hippasus of Metapontum (5th century BCE, middle)
Sophists
Protagoras of Abdera (5th century BCE, middle)
Gorgias of Leontini (5th century BCE, middle)
Thrasymachus of Challedon (5th century BCE, second half)

Classical
Socrates (470–399 BCE)
Plato (c.427–c.347 BCE)
Aristotle (384–322 BCE)
Hellenistic
  Stoics
  Zeno of Citium (c.335–c.264 BCE)
  Cleanthes (304–233 BCE)
  Chrysippus (c.281–c.205 BCE)
  Epicureans
  Epicurus (341–270 BCE)
  Skeptics
  Pyrrho of Elis (c.365–c.275 BCE)
  Sextus Empiricus (3rd century CE, first half)

The philosopher Plato (c.427–347 BCE) was one of Socrates' disciples. Plato disseminated his philosophy through his writing. He also gave classes at a gymnasium dedicated to the hero Academus, on the outskirts of Athens, from which his school, the Academy, took its name.

the development of Greek astronomy illustrate the deductive bias of Greek thought and its characteristic weakness, its urge to set out a plausible theory to account for the widest possible range of experience without submitting it to the test of experiment. It affected most fields of thought which we now think to be covered by science and philosophy. Its fruits were on the one hand argument of unprecedented rigour and acuteness and on the other an ultimate scepticism about sense-data. Only the Greek doctors, led by the fifth-century Hippocrates, made much of empiricism.

PLATO

IN THE CASE of Plato – and, for good or ill, philosophical discussion has been shaped more by him and his pupil Aristotle than by any other two men – this bias may have been reinforced by his low opinion of what he observed. By birth an aristocratic Athenian,

he turned away from the world of practical affairs in which he had hoped to take part, disillusioned with the politics of the Athenian democracy, and, in particular, with its treatment of Socrates, whom it had condemned to death. From Socrates Plato had learnt not only his Pythagoreanism but an idealist approach to ethical questions, and a technique of philosophical enquiry. The Good, he thought, was discoverable by enquiry and intuition; it was reality. It was the greatest of a series of "ideas" – Truth, Beauty, Justice were others – which were not ideas in the sense that at any moment they had shape in anyone's mind (as one might say "I have an idea about that"), but were real entities, enjoying a real existence in a world fixed and eternal, of which such ideas were the elements. This world of changeless reality, thought Plato, was hidden from us by the senses, which deceived us and misled us. But it was accessible to the soul, which could understand it by the use of reason.

Such ideas had a significance going far

beyond technical philosophy. In such ideas (like those of Pythagoras) can be found, for example, traces of a familiar later idea, that of puritanism, that a human being is irreconcilably divided between the soul, of divine origin, and the body which imprisons it. Not reconciliation, but the victory of one or another, must be the outcome. It was an idea which would pass into Christianity with enormous effect. Immediately, Plato had an intensely practical concern since he believed that knowledge of the Ideal world of universals and reality could be helped or hindered by the arrangements under which people lived.

THE REPUBLIC

Plato set out his views in a series of dialogues between Socrates and people who came to argue with him. They were the first textbooks of philosophical thinking and the one we call *The Republic* was the first book in which anyone had ever set out a scheme for a society directed and planned to achieve an ethical goal. It describes an authoritarian state (reminiscent of Sparta) in which marriages would be regulated to produce the best genetic results, families and private property would not exist, culture and the arts would be censored and education carefully supervised. The few who ruled this state would be those of sufficient intellectual and moral stature to fit them for the studies which would enable them to realize the just society in practice by apprehending the Ideal world. Like Socrates, Plato held that wisdom was the understanding of reality and he assumed that to see truth ought to make it impossible not to act in accordance with it. Unlike his teacher, he held that for most people education and the laws should impose exactly that unexamined life which Socrates had thought not worth living. *The Republic* and its arguments were to provoke centuries of discussion and imitation, but this was true of almost all Plato's work. As a twentieth-century English philosopher put it, practically all subsequent

---

Plato's *The Republic*

"... it is obvious that the elder must govern, and the younger be governed."

"That is obvious."

"And again that those who govern must be the best of them."

"That's equally obvious."

"And the best farmers are those who have the greatest skill at farming, are they not?"

"Yes."

"And so if we want to pick the best Guardians, we must pick those who have the greatest skill in watching over the community."

"Yes."

"For that shan't we need men who, besides being intelligent and capable, really care for the community?"

"True."

"But we care most for what we love."

"Inevitably."

"And the deepest affection is based on identity of interest, when we feel that our own good and ill fortune is completely bound up with that of something else."

"That is so."

"So we must choose from among our Guardians those who appear to us on observation to be most likely to devote their lives to doing what they judge to be in the interest of the community, and who are never prepared to act against it."

An extract from Book III of *The Republic* by Plato, translated by Desmond Lee.

philosophy in the West was a series of footnotes to Plato. In spite of Plato's distaste for what he saw about him and the prejudice it engendered in him, he anticipated almost all the great questions of philosophy, whether they concerned morals, aesthetics, the basis of knowledge, or the nature of mathematics, and he set out his ideas in great works of literature, which have always been read with pleasure.

Aristotle (384–322 BCE) founded a philosophical school, the Lyceum, which was attended by a large number of followers. He was also Alexander the Great's tutor.

ARISTOTLE

THE ACADEMY which Plato founded has some claim to be the first university. From it emerged his pupil Aristotle, a thinker more comprehensive and balanced, less sceptical of the possibilities of the actual, and less adventurous than he. Aristotle never altogether rejected his master's teaching but he departed from it in fundamental ways. He was a great classifier and collector of data (with a special interest in biology) and did not reject sense experience as did Plato. Indeed, he sought both firm knowledge and happiness in the world of experience, rejecting the notion of universal ideas and arguing inductively from facts to general laws. Aristotle was so rich a thinker and interested in so many sides of experience that his historical influence is as hard to delimit as that of Plato. What he wrote provided a framework for the discussion of biology, physics, mathematics, logic, literary criticism, aesthetics, psychology, ethics and politics for two thousand years. He provided ways of thinking about these subjects and approaches to them which were elastic and capacious enough eventually to contain Christian philosophy. He also founded a science of deductive logic which

was not displaced until the end of the nineteenth century. It is a vast achievement, different in kind but not less important than that of Plato.

THE MEAN

Aristotle's political thinking was in one sense in agreement with Plato's: the city-state was the best conceivable social form, but required reform and purification to work properly, he thought. But beyond this point he diverged greatly from his master. Aristotle saw the proper working of the *polis* as being that which would give each of its parts the role appropriate to it and that was essentially for him a matter of understanding what led in most existing states to happiness. In formulating an answer, he made use of a Greek idea to which his teaching was to give long life, that of the Mean, the idea that excellence lay in a balance between extremes. The empirical facts seemed to confirm this and Aristotle assembled greater quantities of such evidence in a systematic form than any predecessor, it seems; but in stressing the importance of facts about society, he had been anticipated by another Greek invention, that of history.

The decoration on this ceramic piece depicts an imaginary dialogue between the great philosopher Plato and his student Aristotle.

This scene illustrates an episode from the War of the Titans, a struggle which, according to Greek mythology, was held at the beginning of time between the gods of Olympus and the giants, sons of the Earth. This is one of the most glorious myths related in Hesiod's poetry. Here, it is used as a theme to decorate this frieze from the Great Altar of Zeus and Athene at Pergamum, erected in the 2nd century BCE.

GREEK HISTORIANS

THE INVENTION OF HISTORY was another major achievement. In most countries, chronicles or annals which purport simply to record successions of events precede history. In Greece, this was not so. Historical writing in Greek emerged from poetry. Amazingly, it at once reached its highest level in its first embodiments, two books by masters which were never equalled by their successors.

HERODOTUS

The first Greek historian, Herodotus, has reasonably been termed "the father of history". The word – *historie* – existed before him; it meant enquiry. Herodotus gave it an added meaning, that of enquiry about events in time, and in putting down the results wrote the first prose work of art in a European language which survives. His stimulus was a wish to understand a near-contemporary fact, the great struggle with Persia. He accumulated information about the Persian Wars and their antecedents by reading a huge mass of the available literature and by interrogating people on his travels and assiduously recording what he was told and read. For the first time, these things became the subject of more than a chronicle. The result is his *Histories*, a remarkable account of the Persian Empire, with, built into it, much information about early Greek history and a sort of world survey, followed by an account of the Persian Wars down to Mycale. He spent much of his life travelling, having been born (it was traditionally said) in the Dorian town of Helicarnassus in southwest Asia Minor in 484 BCE. At one point he came to Athens where he remained for a few years living as a metic, and while there he may have been rewarded for public recitations of his work. He went later to a new colony in southern Italy; there he completed his work and died, a little after 430 BCE. He therefore knew something by experience of the whole spread of the Greek world and travelled in Egypt and elsewhere as well. Thus wide experience lay behind his great book, an account scrupulously based on witnesses, even if Herodotus sometimes treated them somewhat credulously.

THUCYDIDES

It is usually conceded that one of the superiorities of Thucydides, Herodotus' greater successor, was his more rigorous approach to reports of fact and his attempts to control them in a critical way. The result is a more impressive intellectual achievement, though its austerity throws into even stronger relief the charm of Herodotus' work. Thucydides' subject was even more contemporary, the Peloponnesian War. The choice reflected deep personal involvement and a new conception. Thucydides was a member of a leading Athenian family (he served as a general until disgraced for an alleged failure in command) and he wanted to discover the causes which had brought his city and Greece into their dreadful plight. He shared with Herodotus a practical motive, for he thought (as most Greek historians were to do after him) that what he found out would have practical value, but he sought not merely to describe, but to explain. The result is one of the most striking pieces of historical analysis ever written and the first ever to seek to penetrate through different levels of explanation. In the process he provided a model of disinterested judgment to future historians, for his Athenian loyalties rarely obtrude. The book was not completed – it takes the story

only to 411 BCE – but the overall judgment is concise and striking: "the growth of Athens' power and Sparta's fear was, in my view, the cause which compelled them to go to war".

The invention of history is itself evidence of the new intellectual range of the literature created by the Greeks. It is the first complete one known to humanity. The Jewish is almost as comprehensive, but contains neither drama nor critical history, let alone the lighter genres. But Greek literature shares with the Bible a primacy shaping the whole of subsequent western writing. Besides its positive

The Great Sphinx of Giza represents a creature with a human head and a lion's body and was constructed in the 3rd millennium BCE. The precise religious significance of the Sphinx when it was erected, during ancient Egypt's Old Empire, remains a mystery. It was linked with the sun god and later came to be identified with the god Horus.

content, it imposed the major forms of literature and the first themes of a criticism by which to judge them.

POETRY AND DRAMA

FROM THE BEGINNING, as Homer shows, Greek literature was closely linked to religious belief and moral teaching. Hesiod, a poet who probably lived in the late eighth century and is usually considered to be the first Greek poet of the post-epic age, consciously addressed himself to the problem of justice and the nature of the gods, thus confirming the tradition that literature was for more than enjoyment and setting out one of the great themes of Greek literature for the next four centuries. For the Greeks, poets were always likely to be seen as teachers, their work suffused with mystical overtones, inspiration. Yet there were to be many poets, many styles of poetry in Greek. The first which can be distinguished is writing in a personal vein which was to the taste of aristocratic society. But as private patronage became concentrated during the era of the tyrants, so it passed slowly into the collective and civic area. The tyrants deliberately fostered the public festivals which were to be vehicles of the greatest specimens of Greek literary art, the tragedies. The drama's origins lie everywhere in religion and its elements must have been present in every civilization. The ritual of worship is the first theatre. Yet there, too, the Greek achievement was to press this towards conscious reflexion on what was going forward; more was to be expected of the audience than passive resignation or orgiastic possession. The didactic impulse emerges in it.

TRAGEDY

The first form of the Greek drama was the dithyramb, the choral song recited at the festivals of Dionysus, together with dance

---

Greek theatre

The origin of Greek tragedy can be found in the Dionysian dithyramb – performances in which choruses sang hymns in honour of the god. The role of the chorus in early Greek drama was very important: plays consisted of a dialogue between one actor and the chorus. Later, the action became more complicated; the number of actors was increased and, in Euripides' plays, the chorus was reduced to separating the main episodes of the tragedy. The range of theatrical effects also widened.

Increasingly, playwrights made an effort to expose the characters' emotions through oratory duels between the protagonists, thus fostering the interest and empathy of the audience. The number of ancient Greek theatres that have survived to the present day suggest that the theatre-going public must have been very large and in Athens annual drama festivals were held, at which writers competed for prizes. Among the greatest of the Greek tragic writers were the famous poets Aeschylus, Sophocles and Euripides.

Comedy developed simultaneously to tragedy and in Athens the genre was eventually taken over by the state. The most significant 5th-century BCE comedy writer, Aristophanes, was followed in the next century by the highly popular comic poet, Menander.

A krater depicting a group of Greek comic actors.

and mime. In 535 BCE, we are told, this was the subject of a crucial innovation, when Thespis added to it an individual actor whose speech was some kind of antiphone to the chorus. Further innovation and more actors followed and within a hundred years we have reached the full, mature theatre of Aeschylus, Sophocles and Euripides. Of their work thirty-three plays survive (including one complete trilogy), but we know that more than three hundred different tragedies were performed in the fifth century. In this drama the religious undertone is still there, though not so much in the words as in the occasions at which they would have been performed. The great tragedies were sometimes performed in trilogies at civic festivals attended by citizens who were already familiar with the basic stories (often mythological) they had come to see. This, too, suggests the educational effect.

Probably most Greeks never saw a play by Aeschylus; certainly an infinitesimally small number by comparison with the number of modern English people who have seen a play of Shakespeare. None the less, those who were not too busy on their farms, or too far away, provided a large audience.

More human beings than in any other ancient society were able to scrutinize and reflect upon the content of their own moral and social world. What they expected was a revealing emphasis in familiar rites, a new selection from their meaning, and this is what the great dramatists mostly gave them, even if some plays went beyond this and some even, at favourable moments, satirized social pieties. It was not, of course, a naturalistic picture that was presented, but the operation of the laws of a heroic, traditional world and their agonizing impact on individuals caught

A 4th-century BCE bronze votive mask of the kind worn by actors performing in tragedies.

This detail is taken from a 4th-century BCE vase by the Greek painter Python. The scene depicts a performance of the *Eumenides*, the third play of the *Oresteia* trilogy, written by the tragic poet Aeschylus.

in their working. In the second half of the fifth century Euripides had even begun to use the conventional tragic form as a vehicle for questioning conventional assumptions; thus he inaugurated a technique to be exploited in the Western theatre by authors as late and as different as Gogol and Ibsen. The framework provided by plot, though, was familiar, and at its heart lay a recognition of the weight of inexorable law and *nemesis*. The acceptance of this setting may be thought, in the last resort, to be testimony to the irrational rather than the rational side of the Greek mind. Yet it was a long way from the state of mind in which the congregation of an eastern temple fearfully or hopefully witnessed the round of unchanging ritual and sacrifice.

COMEDY

In the fifth century the scope of the theatre was broadening in other ways. This was when Attic comedy developed as a form in its own right, and found in Aristophanes its first great manipulator of people and events for others' amusement. His material was often political, almost always highly topical, and frequently scurrilous. His survival and success is the most striking evidence we possess of the tolerance and freedom of Athenian society. A hundred years later, we have almost reached the modern world in a fashion for plays about the intrigues of slaves and troubled love-affairs. It has not the impact of Sophocles, but it can still amuse and remains a near-miracle, for nothing like it had been there two hundred years before. The rapidity with which Greek literature grew after the age of epic poetry and its enduring power is evidence of Greek powers of innovation and mental development which, even when we cannot explain it, we can still appreciate today.

THE VISUAL ARTS

L ITERATURE AT THE END of the classical age still had a long and important life ahead when the city-states disappeared. It had a growing audience, for Greek was to become both *lingua franca* and an official language over all the Near East and much of the Mediterranean. It was not to reach again the heights of Athenian tragedy, but it was still to show us masterpieces. The sense of decline in the visual arts is more apparent. Here, above all in monumental architecture and the nude, Greece had again set standards for the future. From the first borrowings from Asia a wholly original architecture was evolved, the classical style whose elements are still consciously evoked even by the austerities of twentieth-century builders. Within a few hundred years it spread over much of the world from Sicily to India; in this art, too, the Greeks were cultural exporters.

These baked-clay figurines represent actors from a Greek comedy.

MONUMENTAL ARCHITECTURE

The Greeks were in one respect favoured by geology, for Greece contained much high-quality stone. Its durability is attested by the magnificence of the relics we look at today. Yet there is an illusion in this. The purity and austerity with which fifth-century Athens speaks to us in the Parthenon conceals its image in Greek eyes. We have lost the garish statues of gods and goddesses, the paint and ochre and the clutter of monuments, shrines and *stelae* that must have encumbered the Acropolis and obscured the simplicity of its temples. The reality of many great Greek centres may have been more like, say, modern Lourdes; a jumble of untidy little shrines cluttered by traders, booths, and the rubbish of superstition is the impression gained when approaching the Temple of Apollo at Delphi (though we must make allowances for the contribution made by the archaeologist to this impression).

None the less, this qualification made,

Greek architecture

The remains of temples are the most impressive surviving examples of classical Greek architecture. Although each temple tends to have a standard ground plan, the elevation usually belongs to one of the two main orders of Greek architecture, the Doric and the Ionic. At first, the two orders were unevenly distributed in geographical terms: the Doric in mainland Greece, Sicily and southern Italy, and the Ionic in Anatolia and the Aegean islands. Later, from the 5th century BCE onwards, the movement of populations and political affinities between cities allowed greater exchange.

The Doric style, which is more severe, can be primarily distinguished by its baseless columns, which are thinner at the top than at the bottom with very simple capitals. Metope panels above the architrave were sometimes embellished with reliefs. In contrast, the Ionic style is more flamboyant. Columns are set in a decorative base and are more slender with more marked vertical fluting. The main difference can be seen in the capital, which has a double volute, on which rests the architrave, and then a frieze, usually adorned by sculptures.

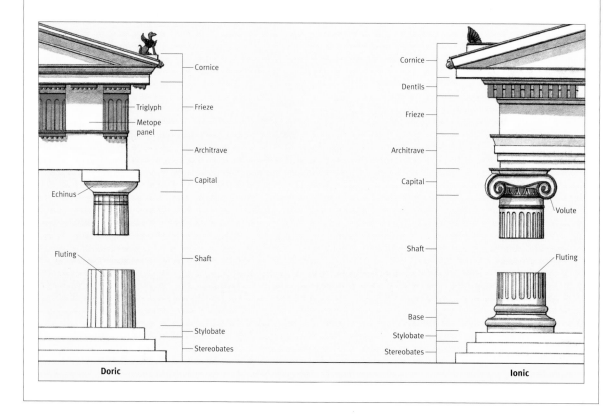

the erosion of time has allowed a beauty of form which is almost unequalled to emerge from the superficial experience. There is no possibility here of discounting the interplay of judgment of the object with standards of judgment which derive ultimately from the object itself. It remains simply true that to have originated an art that has spoken so deeply and powerfully to the human mind across such ages is itself not easily interpreted except as evidence of an unsurpassed artistic greatness and an astonishing skill in giving it expression.

SCULPTURE

Great artistic quality is also present in Greek sculpture. Here, too, the presence of good stone was an advantage, and the original influence of oriental, often Egyptian, models important. Like pottery, the eastern models once absorbed, sculpture evolved towards greater naturalism. The supreme subject of the Greek sculptors was the human form, portrayed no longer as a memorial or cult object, but for its own sake. Again it is not always possible to be sure of the finished statue the Greeks saw; these figures were often gilded, painted or decorated with ivory and precious stones. Some bronzes have undergone looting or melting down, so that the preponderance of stone may itself be misleading. Their evidence, though, records a clear evolution. We begin with statues of gods and of young men and women whose identity is often unknown, simply and symmetrically presented in poses not too far removed from those of the orient. In the classical figures of the fifth century, naturalism begins to tell in an uneven distribution of weight and the abandonment of the simple frontal stance and to evolve towards the mature, human style of Praxiteles and the fourth century in which the body – and for the first time the female nude – is treated.

THE CULTURAL LEGACY

A great culture is more than a mere museum and no civilization can be reduced to a catalogue. For all its élite quality, the achievement and importance of Greece comprehended all sides of life; the politics of the city-state, a tragedy of Sophocles and a statue by Phidias are all part of it. Later ages grasped this intuitively, happily ignorant of the conscientious discrimination which historical scholarship made possible between periods and places. This was a fruitful error, because in the end what Greece was to be thought to be was as important to the future as what she was. The meaning of the Greek experience was to be represented and reinterpreted, and ancient Greece was to be rediscovered and reconsidered and, in different ways, reborn and re-used, for more than two thousand years. For all the ways in which reality had fallen short of later idealization and for all the strength of ties with past, Greek civilization was quite simply the most important

The Parthenon in the Acropolis of Athens is a good example of the Doric order in Greek architecture. It was constructed from Pentelic marble and was built in the middle of the 5th century BCE. Great care was taken over every detail of the structure – for example, the columns lean inward slightly to create an impression of strength and harmony.

extension of humanity's grasp of its own destiny down to that time. Within four centuries, Greece invented philosophy, politics, most of arithmetic and geometry, and the categories of western art. It would be enough, even if her errors, too, had not been so fruitful. Europe has drawn interest on the capital Greece laid down ever since, and through Europe the rest of the world has traded on the same account.

This classical bronze statue of Zeus, god of the sky and supreme deity, was recovered from the sea off Cape Artemisium and was probably made around 460 BCE. The god is preparing to launch a thunderbolt (now missing) from his right hand.

This tombstone, found at Thasos, depicts a dead woman holding a small box which contains a writing scroll. Bas-reliefs carved on tombstones have provided us with a great deal of information about life in ancient Greece.

4 *THE HELLENISTIC WORLD*

THE HISTORY OF GREECE rapidly becomes less interesting after the fifth century. It is also less important. What remains important is the history of Greek civilization and the shape of this, paradoxically, was determined by a kingdom in northern Greece which some said was not Greek at all: Macedon. In the second half of the fourth century it created an empire bigger than any yet seen, the legatee of both Persia and the city-states. It organized the world we call Hellenistic because of the preponderance and uniting force within it of a culture, Greek in inspiration and language. Yet Macedon was a barbarous place, perhaps centuries behind Athens in the quality of its life and culture.

This gold casket was found in the tomb of Philip II of Macedon in the ancient capital of Macedonia, Aegas, now called Vergina. Its decoration includes the star emblem of the Macedonian Dynasty and dates from the 4th century BCE.

THE DECLINE OF PERSIA

The story begins with the decline of Persian power. Persian recovery in alliance with Sparta had masked important internal weaknesses. One of them is commemorated by a famous book, the *Anabasis* of Xenophon, the story of the long march of an army of Greek mercenaries back up the Tigris and across the mountains to the Black Sea after an unsuccessful attempt on the Persian throne by a brother of the king. This was only a minor and subsidiary episode in the important story of Persian decline, an offshoot of one particular crisis of internal division. Throughout the fourth century that empire's troubles continued, province after province (among them Egypt, which won its independence as early as 404 BCE and held it for sixty years) slipping out of control. A major revolt by the western satraps took a long time to master and though in the end imperial rule was restored the cost had been great. When at last reimposed, Persian rule was often weak.

PHILIP OF MACEDON

ONE RULER TEMPTED by the possibilities of the Persian decline was Philip II of Macedon, a not very highly regarded northern state whose power rested on a warrior aristocracy; it was a rough, tough society, its rulers still somewhat like the warlords of Homeric times, their power resting more on personal ascendancy than institutions. Whether this was a state which was a part of the world of the Hellenes was disputed; some Greeks thought Macedonians barbarians, though their kings claimed descent from Greek houses (one going back to Heracles) and their claim was generally recognized. Philip himself sought status; he wanted Macedon to be thought of as Greek. When he became regent of Macedon in 359 BCE he began a steady acquisition of territory at the expense of other Greek states. His ultimate argument was an army which became by the end of his reign the best-trained and organized in Greece. The Macedonian military tradition had emphasized heavy, armoured cavalry, and this continued to be a major arm. Philip added to this tradition the benefit of lessons about infantry he had drawn while a hostage at Thebes in his youth. From hoplite tactics he evolved a new weapon, the sixteen-deep phalanx of pikemen. The men in its ranks carried pikes twice as long as a hoplite spear and they operated in a more open formation, pike shafts from the second and third ranks running between men in the front to present a much denser array of weapons for the charge. Another advantage of the Macedonians was a grasp of siege-warfare techniques not shown by other Greek armies; they had catapults which made it possible to force a besieged town's defenders to take cover while battering-rams, mobile towers and mounds of earth were brought into play. Such things had previously been seen only in the armies of Assyria and their Asian successors. Finally, Philip ruled a fairly wealthy state, its riches much increased once he had acquired the goldmines of Mount Pangaeum, though he spent so much that he left huge debts.

He used his power first to ensure the effective unification of Macedon itself.

Found in Philip II of Macedon's tomb, this small ivory head is thought to be his portrait. The right eye appears to show one of the king's battle scars, said to have resulted from an arrow wound.

Within a few years the infant king for whom he was regent was deposed and Philip was elected king. Then he began to look to the south and northeast. In these areas expansion sooner or later meant encroachment upon the interests and position of Athens. Her allies in Rhodes, Cos, Chios and Byzantium placed themselves under Macedonian patronage. Another, Phocis, went down in a war in which Athens had egged her on but failed to give effective support. Although Demosthenes, the last great agitator of Athenian democracy, made himself a place in history, which is recalled by the word "philippic", by warning his countrymen of

Time chart (359–30 BCE)

359–336 BCE Reign of Philip II of Macedon		**148–145 BCE** Rome annexes Macedonia and Greece	**88–64 BCE** Roman dominion in Asia Minor
300 BCE	**200 BCE**	**100 BCE**	
336–323 BCE Reign of Alexander the Great	**315–301 BCE** Division of Alexander's empire		**30 BCE** Rome annexes Egypt, the last Hellenistic kingdom

The entrance to the Acrocorinth, the great fortress that towered above the ancient city of Corinth, is one of the best surviving examples of Greek military architecture, built in an age when the demise of the *polis* meant that outer defences were necessary. The fortress was connected to the city by long walls in the 4th century BCE.

the dangers they faced, he could not save them. When a war between others and Macedon (355–346 BCE) at last ended, Philip had won not only Thessaly, but had established himself in central Greece and controlled the pass of Thermopylae.

THE LEAGUE OF CORINTH

Philip's situation favoured designs on Thrace and this implied a return of Greek interests towards Persia. One Athenian writer advocated a Hellenic crusade to exploit Persia's weakness (in opposition to Demosthenes, who continued to denounce the Macedonian "barbarian"), and once more plans were made to liberate the Asian cities, a notion attractive enough to bear fruit in a reluctant League of Corinth formed by the major Greek states other than Sparta in 337 BCE. Philip was its president and general, but the apparent independence of its members was a sham, for they were Macedonian satellites. Though the culmination of Philip's work and reign (he was assassinated the following year), it had only come into being after Macedon had defeated the Athenians and Thebans in 338 BCE. The terms of peace imposed by Philip were not harsh, but the League had to agree to go to war with Persia under Macedonian leadership. There was one more kick of Greek independence after Philip's death, but his son and successor Alexander crushed the Greek rebels as he did others in other parts of his kingdom. Thebes was then razed to the ground and its population enslaved (335 BCE).

The Macedonian army

Philip reorganized Macedonia's army, which had been based on a cavalry made up of noblemen. The king increased the number of infantry soldiers, took pains to arm them well and provided them with a new weapon: the *sarissa*, a 20-ft (6-m) long pike (one and a half times as long as the Greek spears). He also created the phalanx, a concentrated infantry group consisting of 16 rows of soldiers. The soldiers in the front five rows lowered their *sarissas* to go into battle. This mass of soldiers was more manoeuvrable than the Greek formations of the day and its weapons easier to handle. Its flanks and rearguard were protected by cavalry.

Reconstruction of a Macedonian phalanx ready to go into battle.

The legendary Alexander

Born in 356 BCE, Alexander studied under the philosopher Aristotle, who instructed him in classical Greek culture and told him stories about the revered heroes of Greek mythology. In 336 BCE, at the age of twenty, Alexander succeeded his father, Philip II. Macedon's new king was a battle-hardened soldier who had already taken part in the conquest of Greece.

The Egyptians' willingness to treat Alexander as a deity had a huge influence on the young man's behaviour. He cultivated his image as a divine being deserving of worship, although it is not known whether he believed himself to be a god. Alexander used carefully orchestrated propaganda techniques to control his public image – he allowed himself to be portrayed only by his own official sculptors.

This typically idealized portrait of Alexander the Great, which was made in Miletus in the first half of the 2nd century BCE, depicts him as a handsome and heroic leader.

ALEXANDER THE GREAT

THE DEFEAT OF THEBES was the real end of four centuries of Greek history. During them civilization had been created and sheltered by the city-state, one of the most successful political forms the world has ever known. The immediate future for Greece was Macedonian governors and garrisons. Not for the first time nor the last, the future seemed to belong to the bigger battalions, the bigger organizations. Mainland Greece was from this time a political backwater. Like his father, Alexander sought to conciliate the Greeks by giving them a large measure of internal self-government in return for adherence to his foreign policy. This was always to leave some Greeks, notably the Athenian democrats, unreconciled. When Alexander died, Athens once more tried to organize an anti-Macedonian coalition. The results were disastrous. A part of the price of defeat was the replacement of democracy by oligarchy at Athens (322 BCE); Demosthenes fled to an island off the coast, seeking sanctuary in the temple of Poseidon there, but poisoned himself when the Macedonians came for him. A Macedonian governor henceforth ruled the Peloponnese.

Alexander's reign had thus begun with difficulties, but once they were surmounted, he could turn his attention to Persia. In 334 BCE he crossed to Asia at the head of an army of which a quarter was drawn from Greece. There was more than idealism in this; aggressive war might also be prudent, for the fine army left by Philip had to be paid if it was not to present a threat to a new king, and conquest would provide the money. He was twenty-two years old and before him lay a short career of conquest so brilliant that it would leave his name a myth down the ages and provide a setting for the widest expansion of Greek culture. He drew the city-states into a still wider world.

CONQUESTS

The story of Alexander's success is simple to summarize. Legend says that after crossing to Asia Minor he cut the Gordian Knot. He then defeated the Persians at the battle of Issus. This was followed by a campaign which swept south through Syria, destroying Tyre on the way, and eventually to Egypt, where Alexander founded the city still bearing his name. In every battle he was his own best soldier and he was wounded several times in the mêlée. He pushed into the desert, interrogated the oracle at Siwah and then went back into Asia to inflict a second and decisive defeat on Darius III in 331 BCE. Persepolis was sacked and burnt and Alexander proclaimed successor to the Persian throne; Darius was murdered by one of his satraps the next year. On went Alexander, pursuing the Iranians of the northeast into Afghanistan (where Kandahar, like many cities elsewhere, commemorates

his name) and penetrating a hundred miles or so beyond the Indus into the Punjab. Then he turned back because his army would go no further. It was tired and having defeated an army with 200 elephants may have been disinclined to face a further 5,000 reported to be waiting for it in the Ganges valley. Alexander returned to Babylon. There he died in 323 BCE, thirty-two years old and just ten years after he had left Macedon.

ALEXANDER THE GREAT'S ACHIEVEMENTS

Both Alexander's conquests and their organization in empire bear the stamp of individual genius; the word is not too strong,

Alexander's march to the east

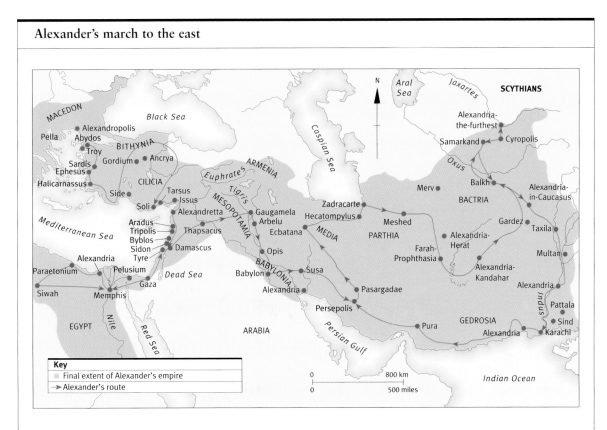

In 334 BCE, Alexander and his army crossed the Dardanelles with the aim of crushing the Persian empire. After crossing Asia Minor and marching along the Mediterranean coast to Egypt, he headed

eastwards. When his army finally mutinied in 323 BCE, Alexander decided to return westwards. However, his journey only took him as far as Babylon, where he died at the age of 32, possibly the victim of a plague.

for achievement on this scale is more than the fruit of good fortune, favourable historical circumstance or blind determinism. Alexander was a creative mind, but self-absorbed, obsessed with his pursuit of glory, and something of a visionary. With great intelligence he combined almost reckless courage; he believed his mother's ancestor to be Homer's Achilles and strove to emulate the hero. He was ambitious as much to prove himself in men's eyes – or perhaps those of his forceful and repellent mother – as to win new lands. The idea of the Hellenic crusade against Persia undoubtedly had reality for him, but he was also, for all his admiration of the Greek culture of which he had learnt from his tutor Aristotle, too egocentric to be a missionary, and his cosmopolitanism was grounded in an appreciation of realities. His empire had to be run by Persians as well as Macedonians. Alexander himself married first a Bactrian and then a Persian princess, and accepted – unfittingly, thought some of his companions – the homage which the East rendered to rulers it thought to be godlike. He was also at times rash and impulsive; it was his soldiers who finally made him turn back at the Indus, and the ruler of Macedon had no business to plunge into battle with no attention for what would happen to the monarchy if he should die without a successor. Worse still, he killed a friend in a drunken brawl and he may have arranged his father's murder.

Alexander lived too short a time either to ensure the unity of his empire in the future or to prove to posterity that even he could not have held it together for long. What he did in this time is indubitably impressive. The foundation of twenty-five "cities" is by itself a considerable matter, even if some of them were only spruced-up strongpoints; they were keys to the Asian land routes. The integration of east and west in their government was still more difficult, but Alexander took it a long

way in ten years. Of course, he had little choice; there were not enough Greeks and Macedonians to conquer and govern the huge empire. From the first he ruled through Persian officials in the conquered areas and after coming back from India he began the reorganization of the army in mixed regiments of Macedonians and Persians. His adoption of Persian dress and his attempt to exact prostration – an obligatory kow-tow like that which so many Europeans in recent times found degrading when it was asked for by Chinese rulers – from his compatriots as

well as from Persians, also antagonized his followers, for they revealed his taste for oriental manners. There were plots and mutinies; they were not successful, and his relatively mild reprisals do not suggest that the situation was ever very dangerous for Alexander. The crisis was followed by his most spectacular gesture of cultural integration when, himself taking Darius' daughter as a wife (in addition to his Bactrian princess, Roxana), he then officiated at the mass wedding of 9,000 of his soldiers to eastern women. This was the famous "marriage of East and West", an act of state rather than of idealism, for the new empire had to be cemented together if it was to survive.

What the empire really meant in cultural interplay is more difficult to assess. There was certainly a wider physical dispersal of Greeks. But the results of this were only to appear after Alexander's death, when the formal framework of empire collapsed and yet the cultural fact of a Hellenistic world emerged from it. We do not in fact know very much about life in Alexander's empire and it must be unlikely, given its brief duration, the

This detail of the so-called Alexander mosaic from Pompeii depicts a battle between Alexander the Great and the Persian king Darius III. Dating from the 2nd century BCE, the mosaic is a replica of a late 4th-century BCE Greek fresco. The figure represents Alexander entering the fray.

This bas-relief comes from the famous so-called Alexander sarcophagus, made in 305 BCE in painted marble, and decorated on this side with battle scenes that are much more realistic than usual for the classical period. Alexander is shown on the left on horseback, wearing a lion-scalp helmet.

An effigy of Ptolemy I (305–282 BCE) is displayed on this coin. A Greek general in Alexander the Great's army, Ptolemy Soter later became King Ptolemy I of Egypt. He founded the Ptolemaic Dynasty, which ruled until the Roman conquest of Egypt at the end of the 1st century BCE.

limitations of ancient government and a lack of will to embark upon fundamental change, that most of its inhabitants found things very different in 323 BCE from what they had been ten years before.

ALEXANDER'S LEGACY

Alexander's impact was made in the east. He did not reign long enough to affect the interplay of the western Greeks with Carthage which was the main preoccupation of the later fourth century in the west. In Greece itself things stayed quiet until his death. It was in Asia that he ruled lands no Greeks had ruled before. In Persia he had proclaimed himself heir to the Great King and rulers in the northern satrapies of Bithynia, Cappadocia and Armenia did him homage.

Weak as the cement of the Alexandrine Empire must have been, it was submitted to intolerable strain when he died without a competent heir. His generals fell to fighting for what they could get and keep, and the empire was dissolving even before the birth of his posthumous son by Roxana. She had already murdered his second wife, so when she and her son died in the troubles any hope of direct descent vanished. In forty-odd years of fighting it was settled that there would be no reconstitution of Alexander's empire. There emerged instead in the end a group of big states, each of them a hereditary monarchy. They were founded by successful soldiers, the *diadochi*, or "Successors".

THE HELLENISTIC STATES

PTOLEMY SOTER, one of Alexander's best generals, had at once seized power in Egypt at his master's death and to it he subsequently conveyed the valuable prize of Alexander's body. Ptolemy's descendants were to rule the province for nearly three hundred years until the death of Cleopatra in 30 BCE. Ptolemaic Egypt was the longest-lived and richest of the successor states. Of the Asian Empire, the Indian territories and some of Afghanistan passed out of Greek hands altogether, being ceded to an Indian ruler in return for military help. The rest of it was by 300 BCE a huge kingdom of one and a half million square miles and perhaps thirty million subjects, stretching from Afghanistan to Syria, the site of its capital, Antioch. This vast domain was ruled by the descendants of Seleucus, another Macedonian general. Attacks by migrating Celts from northern Europe (who had already invaded Macedonia itself) led to its partial disruption early in the third century BCE and part of it thenceforth

formed the kingdom of Pergamon, ruled by a dynasty called the Attalids, who pushed the Celts further into Asia Minor. The Seleucids kept the rest, though they were to lose Bactria in 225 BCE, where descendants of Alexander's soldiers set up a remarkable Greek kingdom. Macedon, under another dynasty, the Antigonids, strove to retain a control of the Greek states contested in the Aegean by the Ptolemaic fleet and in Asia Minor by the Seleucids. Once again, about 265 BCE, Athens made a bid for independence but failed.

These events are complicated, but not very important for our purpose. What

The Hellenistic world soon after 200 BCE

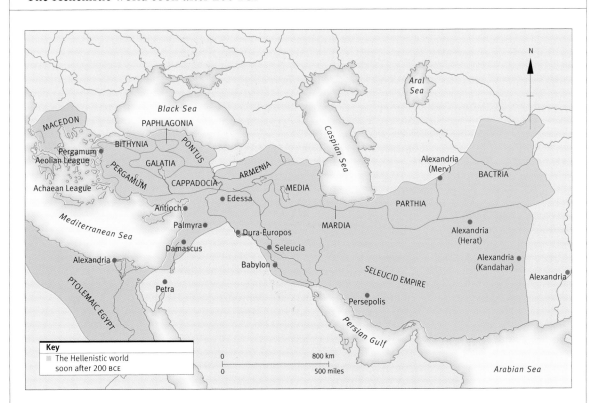

When Alexander the Great died, his generals began to fight for control of his empire's different regions. These disputes left the empire fragmented, making way for the Hellenistic kingdoms. At the beginning of the 3rd century BCE, three large kingdoms were consolidated: Egypt under the Ptolemaic Dynasty;

Syria, Mesopotamia and part of Persia under the Seleucids; and Macedonia under the Antigonid Dynasty. Later, the borders of these kingdoms were altered and some minor kingdoms appeared. All of them later succumbed to pressure from the Romans and the Parthians in the 2nd century BCE.

Hellenism and the city of Pergamum

The Hellenistic period began when Alexander the Great died and ended with the Roman conquest of Asia Minor, which took place throughout the 2nd and 1st centuries BCE. Through the Hellenistic kingdoms founded after Alexander's death, Greek culture spread across the Near East and Egypt, and shifted its main focus outside Greece for the first time. The main centres of Hellenism were generally new Greek colonies and cities, such as Pergamum. In these colonies, a busy cultural life developed and considerable advances were made in the fields of science and art. Greek culture itself was enriched in many ways by oriental influences, notably in politics, art and religion.

The kingdom of Pergamum on the Asian coast became independent from the Seleucid state in the 3rd century BCE and during the following century its capital was a major centre of Hellenistic art and culture. The city was redesigned and adapted to steep, uneven mountainside terrain, its buildings and open spaces linked by a network of stairways and terraces.

Key	
1	Arsenal
2	Temple of Trajan
3	Library
4	Palace
5	Sanctuary of Athene
6	Theatre
7	Great Altar
8	Stoa
9	Upper Agora
10	Sanctuary of Demeter
11	Baths
12	Upper gymnasium
13	Middle gymnasium
14	Lower gymnasium
15	Lower Agora
16	Town wall

(Right) A plan of the Hellenistic city of Pergamum.

(Below) From the year 400 BCE, Pergamum had one of the main sanctuaries dedicated to Asclepius, the Greek god responsible for curing the sick.

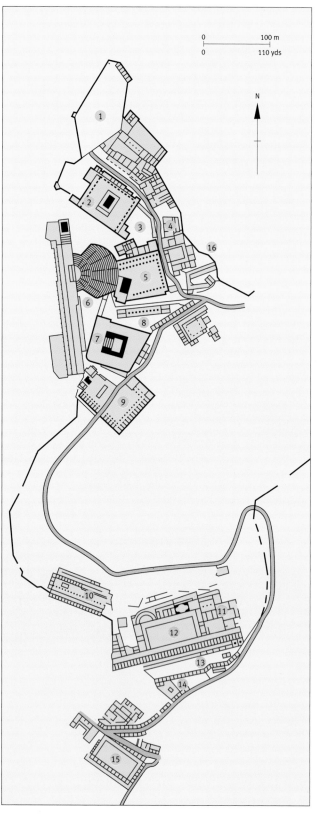

mattered more was that for about sixty years after 280 BCE the Hellenistic kingdoms lived in a rough balance of power, preoccupied with events in the eastern Mediterranean and Asia and, except for the Greeks and Macedonians, paying little attention to events further west. This provided a peaceful setting for the greatest extension of Greek culture and this is why these states are important. It is their contribution to the diffusion and growth of a civilization that constitute their claim on our attention, not the obscure politics and unrewarding struggles of the *diadochi*.

THE HELLENISTIC CITIES

Greek was now the official language of the whole Near East; even more important, it was the language of the cities, the foci of the new world. Under the Seleucids the union of Hellenistic and oriental civilization to which Alexander may have aspired began to be a reality. They urgently sought Greek immigrants and founded new cities wherever they could as a means of providing some solid framework for their empire and of hellenizing the local population. The cities were the substance of Seleucid power, for beyond them stretched a heterogeneous hinterland of tribes, Persian satrapies, vassal princes. Seleucid administration was still based fundamentally upon the satrapies; the theory of absolutism was inherited by the Seleucid kings from the Achaemenids just as was their system of taxation. Yet it is not certain what this meant in practice and the east seems to have been less closely governed than Mesopotamia and Asia Minor, where Hellenistic influence was strongest and the capital lay. The size of the Hellenistic cities here far surpassed those of the older Greek emigrations; Alexandria, Antioch and the

new capital city, Seleucia, near Babylon, quickly achieved populations of between one and two hundred thousand.

This reflected economic growth as well as conscious policy. The wars of Alexander and his successors released an enormous booty, much of it in bullion, accumulated by the Persian Empire. It stimulated economic life all over the Near East, but also brought the evils of inflation and instability. Nevertheless, the overall trend was towards greater wealth. There were no great innovations, either in manufacture or in the tapping of new natural resources. The Mediterranean economy remained much what it had always been except in scale, but Hellenistic civilization was richer than its predecessors and population growth was one sign of this.

Its wealth sustained governments of some magnificence, raising large revenues and spending them in spectacular and

In this late 2nd-century BCE bas-relief, known as *The Apotheosis of Homer*, the poet appears at the bottom left, seated on a throne. Led by Myth and History and accompanied by Physics and Nature, the dramatic genres advance towards Homer to make a sacrifice in his honour, while in the upper section, Zeus and Apollo are depicted with the muses. Sculpted by Archilochus of Pirene, the bas-relief reflects the developing interest in literature in the Hellenistic kingdoms.

A detail from the western part of a frieze that decorates the Great Altar at Pergamum. These dynamic sculptures depict the battle between the gods and the giants.

sometimes commendable ways. The ruins of the Hellenistic cities show expenditure on the appurtenances of Greek urban life; theatres and gymnasia abound, games and festivals were held in all of them. This probably did not much affect the native populations of the countryside who paid the taxes and some of them resented what would now be called "westernization". None the less, it was a solid achievement. Through the cities the east was Hellenized in a way which lasted until the coming of Islam. Soon they produced their own Greek literature.

Yet though this was a civilization of Greek cities, it was in spirit unlike that of the

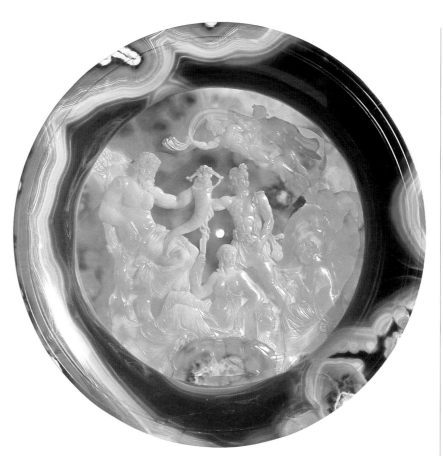

Archimedes

One of the greatest of the Greek mathematicians, Archimedes (c.287–212 BCE) was born in Syracuse and studied in Alexandria. He invented siege engines for use against the Romans and the Archimedean screw, which was used for raising water. He also formulated the famous principle according to which a body submerged in a liquid undergoes an apparent loss of weight equal to the weight of the displaced liquid. Archimedes made many contributions to geometry, calculating the approximate value of *pi*, as well as formulae for working out the area and volume of various figures, including cylinders, spheres and parabolas.

Archimedes was killed by a Roman soldier during the siege of Syracuse, as depicted in this copy of a 2nd-century Roman mosaic.

past, as some Greeks noted sourly. The Macedonians had never known the life of the city-state and their creations in Asia lacked its vigour; the Seleucids founded scores of cities but maintained the old autocratic and centralized administration of the satrapies above that level. Bureaucracy was highly developed and self-government languished. Ironically, besides having to bear the burden of disaster in the past, the cities of Greece itself, where a flickering tradition of independence lived on, were the one part of the Hellenistic world which actually underwent economic and demographic decline.

Dating from 172 BCE, this Alexandrian cameo is one of the few surviving examples of the cultural confluence of Greece and Egypt. It represents the fertility of the Nile. At the bottom of the cameo, the sphinx of Osiris, the Egyptian god of agriculture, appears with the facial features of Ptolemy V.

HELLENISTIC ACADEMIC LIFE

Although the political nerve had gone, city culture still served as a great transmission system for Greek ideas. Large endowments provided at Alexandria and Pergamum the two greatest libraries of the ancient world. Ptolemy I also founded the Museum, a kind of institute of advanced study. In Pergamum a king endowed schoolmasterships and it was there that people perfected the use of parchment (*pergamene*) when the Ptolemies cut off supplies of papyrus. In Athens the Academy and the Lyceum survived and from such sources the tradition of Greek intellectual activity was everywhere refreshed. Much of this activity was academic in the narrow sense that it was in essence commentary on past achievement, but much of it was also of high quality and now seems lacking in weight only because of the gigantic achievements of the fifth and fourth centuries. It was a tradition solid enough to endure right through the Common Era, though much of its content has been irretrievably lost. Eventually, the world of Islam would receive the teaching of Plato and Aristotle through what had been passed on by Hellenistic scholars.

HELLENISTIC SCIENCE

Hellenistic civilization preserved the Greek tradition in nothing more successfully than in science, and here Alexandria, the greatest of all Hellenistic cities, was pre-eminent. Euclid was the greatest systematizer of geometry, defining it until the nineteenth century, and Archimedes, who is famous for his practical achievements in the construction of war-machines in Sicily, was probably Euclid's pupil. Another Alexandrian, Eratosthenes, was the first man to measure the size of the earth, and yet another, Hero, is said to have invented a steam engine and certainly used steam to transmit energy. It is inconceivable that the state of contemporary metallurgy could ever have made the widespread application of this discovery practicable, which probably explains why we hear no more of it.

The point is of general relevance; the intellectual achievements of the ancient world (and of European medieval civilization later) often pushed up to the limits of existing technical skills but could not be expected to go beyond them; further progress had to wait for better instrumentation. Another Hellenistic Greek, Aristarchus of Samos, got so far as to say that the earth moved round the sun, though his views were set aside by contemporaries and posterity because they could not be squared with Aristotelian physics which stated the contrary; the truth or falsity of both views remained untested experimentally. In hydrostatics, it is true, Archimedes made great strides (and invented the windlass, too) but the central achievement of the Greek tradition was always mathematical, not practical, and in Hellenistic times it reached its apogee with the theory of conic sections and ellipses and the founding of trigonometry.

CHANGING POLITICAL STRUCTURES

Such scientific discoveries were important additions to humanity's toolkit. Yet they were less distinct from what went before than was Hellenistic moral and political philosophy. It is tempting to find the reason for this in the political change from the city-state to larger units. It was still in Athens that the philosophy of the age found its greatest centre and Aristotle had hoped to reinvigorate the city-state; in the right hands, he thought, it could still provide the framework for the good life. The unhappy last age of the city-state after the Peloponnesian War and the size and impersonality of the new monarchies must have soon sapped such confidence. In them, the old patriotic impulse of the city-states had dried up. Efforts were made to find other ways of harnessing public loyalty and

The 3rd-century BCE philosopher Chrysippus was a disciple of Zeno and one of the founders of the Stoic school, which became highly influential in the Hellenistic world and later in Rome.

Situated to the southeast of the Athenian Acropolis is the temple of the Olympian, Zeus. Building work on the structure began under Antiochus IV in about 174 BCE and was completed under the Roman emperor Hadrian in the 2nd century CE. The original building had eight columns on its façades, three rows deep, and twenty columns on each side.

emotion. Perhaps because of the need to impress non-Greeks, perhaps because they felt the positive attraction of the world beyond Greek culture, the new monarchs buttressed themselves more and more with oriental cults attached to the person of the ruler whose origins went back into the Mesopotamian and Egyptian past. Extravagant titles were employed but perhaps much of this was flattery: "Soter", as Ptolemy I was called, meant "Saviour". The Seleucids allowed themselves to be worshipped, but the Ptolemies outdid them; they took over the divine status and prestige of the pharaohs (and practice, too, to the extent of marrying their sisters). Meanwhile, the real basis of the Hellenistic states was bureaucracy unchecked by traditions of civic independence – since the Seleucids had founded or refounded most of the Greek cities in Asia, what they had given they could take back – and armies of Greek and Macedonian mercenaries which relieved them of dependence on native troops. Powerful and awe-inspiring though they might be, there was little in such structures to capture their very mixed subjects' loyalties and emotions.

HELLENISTIC RELIGION

Probably the erosion of Hellenistic loyalties had gone too far even before Alexander. The triumph of Greek culture was deceptive. Language went on being used, but with a different meaning. Greek religion, for example, a great force for unity among Hellenes, rested not on ecclesiastical institutions but on respect for the Homeric gods and goddesses and the behaviour they exemplified. Beyond this, there were the city cults and official mysteries. This had already begun to change, possibly as early as the fifth century, when,

under the impact of the prolonged war, the Olympian gods began to lose the respect paid to them. There was more than one cause of this. The rationalism of much Greek fourth-century philosophy is as much a part of the story as the rise of new fears. With the Hellenistic age another influence is felt, that of a pervasive irrationality, of the pressure of fortune and fate. People sought reassurance in new creeds and faiths. The popularity of astrology was one symptom. All this only came to its climax in the first century BCE, "the period", says one scholar, "when the tide of rationalism, which for the past hundred years had flowed ever more sluggishly, has finally expended its force and begins to retreat". This is perhaps further ahead than we need look at this point in the story, but one thing about this reversal is striking at an early date. Swamped as the Hellenistic world was with mysteries and crazes of all kinds, from the revival of Pythagorean mysticism to the raising of altars to dead philosophers, traditional Greek religion was not a beneficiary. Its decay had already gone too far. The decline of Delphi, remarked from the third century, was not arrested.

THE CYNICS AND STOICS

THE COLLAPSE OF A TRADITIONAL religious framework of values was the background to philosophical change. The study of philosophy was still vigorous in Greece itself and even there its Hellenistic development suggests that men were falling back upon personal concerns, contracting out of societies they could not influence, seeking shelter from the buffets of fate and the strain of daily life. It seems somewhat familiar. One example was Epicurus, who sought the good in an essentially private experience of pleasure. Contrary to later misinterpretations, he

A bust of the philosopher Epicurus, who was born on the island of Samos in 341 BCE.

This coin bears the portrait of the Parthian king, Mithridates I (171–138 BCE). He captured Iran from the Seleucids and established the frontier with the Hellenistic kingdom along the Euphrates River.

meant by this something far from self-indulgence. For Epicurus, pleasure was psychological contentment and the absence of pain – a view of pleasure somewhat austere to modern eyes. But symptomatically its importance is considerable because it reveals a shift in people's preoccupations towards the private and personal. Another form of this philosophic reaction advocated the ideals of renunciation and non-attachment. The school known as the Cynics expressed contempt for convention and sought release from dependence on the material world. One of them, Zeno, a Cypriot, who lived at Athens, began to teach a doctrine of his own in a public place, the *stoa Poikile*. The place gave its name to those he taught, the Stoics. They were to be among the most influential of philosophers because their teaching was readily applicable to daily life. Essentially the Stoics taught that life should be lived to fit the rational order they discerned running through the universe. Man could not control what happened to him, they said, but he could accept what was sent by fate, the decree of the divine will in which the Stoics believed. Virtuous acts, accordingly, should not be performed for their likely consequences, which might well be unfortunate or thwarted, but for their own sake, because of their intrinsic value.

THE SUCCESS OF STOICISM

In stoicism, which was to have great success in the Hellenistic world, lay doctrine which gave the individual a new ground for ethical confidence at a time when neither *polis* nor traditional Greek religion retained their authority. Stoicism also had the potential for a long life, because it applied to all men, who, it taught, were all alike: this was the seed of an ethical universalism which gradually transcended the old distinction between Greek and barbarian, as it would any other distinction between reasonable men. It spoke to a common humanity and actually produced a condemnation of slavery, an amazing step in a world built by forced labour. It was to be a fecund source for thinkers for two thousand years. Soon its ethic of disciplined common sense was to have great success at Rome.

The seven wonders of the ancient world

The 30-m (100-ft) high Colossus of Rhodes was an impressive example of the influence that the monumental statues of the East had on Greek sculpture. One Hellenistic citizen considered the Colossus to be one of "the seven things worthy of being seen". Sadly, of these seven ancient "wonders", only the pyramids of Giza survive today.

Key	
1	Statue of Zeus at Olympia
2	Temple of Artemis at Ephesus
3	Mausoleum of Halicarnassus
4	Colossus of Rhodes
5	Pharos of Alexandria
6	Pyramids of Giza
7	Hanging Gardens of Babylon

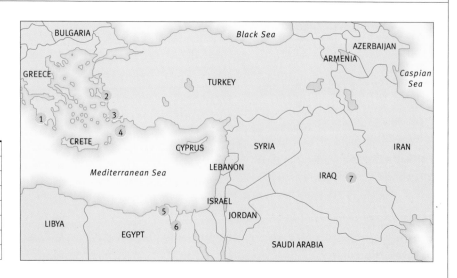

Philosophy thus showed the eclecticism and cosmopolitanism which strike the eye in almost every aspect of Hellenistic culture. Perhaps their most obvious expression was the adaptation of Greek sculpture to the monumental statuary of the East which produced such monsters as the hundred-foot-high Colossus of Rhodes; yet in the end eclecticism and cosmopolitanism appeared every-where, in the aspirations of the Stoics just as in the oriental cults which displaced the Greek gods. It was the scientist Eratosthenes who said that he saw all good men as fellow-countrymen and the remark expresses the new spirit which was Hellenism at its best.

PARTHIA

THE POLITICAL FRAMEWORK of the Hellenistic world was bound in the end to change, because sources of change grew up beyond its circumference. One early omen was the appearance of a new threat in the east, the kingdom of Parthia. By the middle of the third century BCE the weakness imposed by the Seleucid kingdom's concentration of population and wealth in its western half was leading to over-preoccupation with relations with the other Hellenistic states. The northeast was threatened – as always – by nomads from the steppes, but government was distracted from this danger by the need to supply money and resources for quarrels with Ptolemaic Egypt. The temptation to a remote satrap to strike out on his own as a warlord was often irresistible. Scholars contest the details, but one of the satrapies in which this happened was Parthia, an important area to the southeast of the Caspian. It was to become more important still as the centuries passed for it lay across the caravan route to Central Asia by which the western classical world and

These monumental heads belonged to statues of divinities which spread over the terraces marking the tumulus of Nimrud Dagh. Antiochus I ordered the monument to be built in the first half of the 1st century BCE to house the tomb of his father, Mithridates I, who founded the small Commagene kingdom (present-day Turkey).

China came to be remotely in touch, the Silk Road.

PARTHIAN ORIGINS

Who were the Parthians? They were originally the Parni, one of those Indo-European nomadic peoples who emerged from Central Asia to create and re-create a political unity in the highlands of Iran and Mesopotamia. They became a byword for a military skill then peculiar to them: the discharging of arrows by mounted horsemen. They did not build nearly five hundred years of political continuity only on this, though. They also inherited an administrative structure which the Seleucids were left by Alexander, who had taken it from the Persians. Indeed, in most things the Parthians seemed inheritors, not originators; their great dynasty used Greek for its official documents, and they seem to have had no law of their own but to have readily accepted existing practice, whether Babylonian, Persian or Hellenistic.

THE PARTHIAN STATE

Much about the Parthians' early history remains obscure. There was a kingdom, whose centre remains undiscovered, in Parthia in the third century BCE, but the Seleucids do not seem to have reacted strongly to it. In the second century, when the Seleucid monarchy was much more disastrously engaged in the west, two brothers, the younger of whom was Mithridates I, established a Parthian empire which at his death stretched from Bactria (another fragment of the Seleucid inheritance which had been finally separated from it at about the same time as Parthia) in the east to Babylonia in the west. Consciously reminiscent of those who had gone before, Mithridates described himself on his coins as the "great king". There were setbacks after his death but his namesake Mithridates II recovered lost ground and went even further. The Seleucids were now confined to Syria. In Mesopotamia the frontier of his empire was the Euphrates and the Chinese opened diplomatic relations

Syracuse, which became the most powerful Sicilian city, was a Corinthian colony founded in 733 BCE. This theatre probably dates from the 3rd century BCE and has an enormous stage cut into the rock.

with him. The coins of the second Mithridates bore the proud Achaemenid title, "King of Kings", and the inference is reasonable that the Arsacid Dynasty to which Mithridates belonged was now being consciously related to the great Persian line. Yet the Parthian state seems a much looser thing than the Persian. It is more reminiscent of a feudal grouping of nobles about a warlord than a bureaucratized state.

THE GREEK WEST

On the Euphrates, Parthia was eventually to meet a new power from the West. Less remote from it than Parthia and therefore with less excuse, even the Hellenistic kingdoms had been almost oblivious of the rise of Rome, this new star of the political firmament, and went their way almost without regard for what was happening in the West. The western Greeks, of course, knew more about it, but they long remained preoccupied with the first great threat they had faced, Carthage, a mysterious state which almost may be said to have derived its being from hostility to the Greeks. Founded by Phoenicians somewhere about 800 BCE, perhaps even then to offset Greek commercial competition on the metal routes, Carthage had grown to surpass Tyre and Sidon in wealth and power. But she long remained a city-state, using alliance and protection rather than conquests and garrisons, her citizens preferring trade and agriculture to fighting. Unfortunately, the native documentation of Carthage was to perish when, finally, the city was razed to the ground and we know little of its own history.

Yet it was clearly a formidable commercial competitor for the western Greeks. By 480 BCE these had been confined commercially to little more than the Rhône valley, Italy and, above all, Sicily. This island, and

In order to demonstrate that he is of noble birth, this Roman patrician is depicted holding busts of his forefathers. The statue dates from the late 1st century BCE.

one of its cities, Syracuse, was the key to the Greek west. Syracuse for the first time protected Sicily from the Carthaginians when she fought and beat them in the year of Salamis. For most of the fifth century Carthage troubled the western Greeks no more and the Syracusans were able to turn to supporting the Greek cities of Italy against the Etruscans. Then Syracuse was the target of the ill-fated Sicilian Expedition from Athens (415–413 BCE) because she was the greatest of the western Greek states. The Carthaginians came back after this, but Syracuse survived defeat

The Mediterranean in 600 BCE

The movement of colonists from the Greek *polis* and the Phoenician cities in search of lands in the central and western Mediterranean encouraged the creation of new colonies, which in turn became important trade centres. The Phoenician settlement in Carthage is a good example of this.

A map showing the main Mediterranean colonies in 600 BCE.

to enjoy soon afterwards her greatest period of power, exercised not only in the island, but in southern Italy and the Adriatic. During most of it she was at war with Carthage. There was plenty of vigour in Syracuse; at one moment she all but captured Carthage, and another expedition added Corcyra (Corfu) to her Adriatic possessions. But soon after 300 BCE it was clear that Carthaginian power was growing while Syracuse had also to face a Roman threat in mainland Italy. The Sicilians fell out with a man who might have saved them, Pyrrhus of Epirus, and by mid-century the Romans were masters of the mainland.

THE POWER OF HELLENIZATION

There were now three major actors in the arena of the West, yet the Hellenistic east seemed strangely uninterested in what was going forward (though Pyrrhus was aware of it). This was perhaps short-sighted, but at this time the Romans did not see themselves as world conquerors. They were as much moved by fear as by greed in entering on the Punic Wars, from which they would emerge victors. Then they would turn east. Some Hellenistic Greeks were beginning to be aware by the end of the century of what might be coming. A "cloud in the west" was one description of the struggle between Carthage and Rome viewed from the Hellenized east. Whatever its outcome, this struggle was bound to have great repercussions for the whole Mediterranean. None the less, the East was to prove in the event that it had its own strengths and powers of resistance. As one Roman later put it, Greece would take her captors captive, Hellenizing yet more barbarians.

This 1st-century BCE sculpture, *Laocoön and his Sons*, shows the story of the lapsed priest of Apollo at Troy, who advised the Trojans not to bring the Greeks' wooden horse into the city. While the priest was preparing to sacrifice to Poseidon, two serpents strangled him and his children.

Aryan penetration into
the Indus valley begins

1700–1200 BCE
Hittite kingdom

| **1750 BCE** | **1700 BCE** | **1650 BCE** |

2250–1750 BCE saw the zenith of the
Harappan civilization, centred around the
cities of Harappa and Mohenjo-Daro in
the Indus valley. Around 2,500 Harappan
seals have been found in the area.

Harappan seal depicting a buffalo

1353–1336 BCE
The reign of Akhnaton,
who established monotheist
worship in Egypt

| **1450 BCE** | **1400 BCE** | **1350 BCE** |

Ancient Chinese vase

This bronze lid from a ritual vase
depicts a stylized animal head and
dates from the period of the Western
Chou. The Chou dynasty ruled China
until c.256 BCE.

| **1150 BCE** | **1100 BCE** | **1050 BCE** |

800–450 BCE
Hallstatt culture is Europe's
first Iron Age culture

776 BCE
First Olympian games: date from
which Greek calendar begins

| **850 BCE** | **800 BCE** | **750 BCE** |

753 BCE
The legendary
foundation of Rome

The Greek goddess of love, Aphrodite, was
one of the twelve Olympian gods. This 5th-
century BCE marble plaque depicting her
birth shows Aphrodite emerging from the
foaming sea, assisted by her handmaidens,
the Graces and the Seasons.

The birth of Aphrodite

c.484–c.430 BCE
Life of Herodotus,
first Greek historian

c.460–370 BCE
Life of Hippocrates,
Greek doctor

431–404 BCE
The Peloponnesian
War

c.563–483 BCE
Life of the Buddha

| **550 BCE** | **500 BCE** | **450 BCE** |

559–529 BCE
Reign of Persian
emperor Cyrus II

551–479 BCE
Life of Confucius,
Chinese philosopher

525–456 BCE
Life of Aeschylus,
Greek dramatist

500–479 BCE
Median wars: Greek
victory over Persia

460–400 BCE
Life of Thucydides,
Greek historian

At the end of the period of the Warring States,
the Ch'in dominated the other states and their
king became the first emperor of China. Known
as Shih Huang-ti, he ruled from 221 BCE until
206 BCE. His mausoleum was guarded by
thousands of life-size terracotta figures.

Figure from Shih Huang-ti's mausoleum

c.287–212 BCE
Life of Archimedes of Syracuse,
Hellenistic physicist

148–145 BCE
Rome annexes
Macedonia and Greece

| **250 BCE** | **200 BCE** | **150 BCE** |

341–270 BCE
Life of Epicurus of Samos,
Hellenistic philosopher

202 BCE
Reunification of China
by the Han dynasty

*Mithridates I
portrayed on a coin*

The Parthian king Mithridates I (171–138
BCE) won Iran from the Seleucids and
established his kingdom's frontier along
the Euphrates river.

Fall of the Harappan
civilization in the Indus valley

3500–1500 BCE
Megalithic constructions
in Europe

1600 BCE   1550 BCE   1500 BCE

1600–1200 BCE
Mycenean civilization
in Greece

1539–1075 BCE
Egyptian New Kingdom

1500–1000 BCE
Composition of the
Vedic hymns in India

1300–800 BCE
Urnfield cultures in Europe

1220 BCE
Destruction of Troy

1300 BCE   1250 BCE   1200 BCE

1290–1224 BCE
Reign of Ramses II of Egypt

Hebrew exodus from Egypt

The Olmec culture in Mexico, which lasted from
1200 to 400 BCE, represented the beginning of
the great Mesoamerican tradition. This colossal
head is one of eight such basalt figures found
at a ceremonial site and thought to represent
important Olmec rulers.

Olmec carved figure

1000 BCE   950 BCE   900 BCE

Doric invasion of Greece
Ionian emigration to Asia Minor

Statuette of Lao Tzu

Lao Tzu (604–531 BCE), the
legendary founder of Taoism, is
thought to be the author of a
book of aphorisms called the
Tao-te Ching.

Greek colonization
begins in the Mediterranean
The Greek alphabet appears

700 BCE   650 BCE   600 BCE

640–546 BCE
The life of Thales, first
Greek philosopher

612 BCE
Medes and Babylonians
conquer Assyria

Macedonian gold casket

Philip II of Macedonia, who reigned from
359–336 BCE, was the conqueror of Greece.
This gold casket, found in his tomb, is
decorated with the star emblem of the
Macedonian dynasty.

c.427–347 BCE
Life of Plato, Greek
philosopher

323–283 BCE
Life of Euclid, Hellenistic
mathematician

384–322 BCE
Life of Aristotle,
Greek philosopher

400 BCE   350 BCE   300 BCE

315–301 BCE
The division of
Alexander's empire

This Roman bust portrays one of the
most celebrated of the ancient Greek
philosophers, Socrates, who lived in
Athens from 470 BCE to 399 BCE. Because
Socrates did not record anything in
writing, his teachings have come down to
us through the works of his disciple, Plato.

Bust of Socrates

Alexander the Great of Macedonia,
who ruled between 336 and 323 BCE,
conquered the Persian Empire. This
detail from the so-called "Alexander
mosaic" from Pompeii depicts
Alexander going into battle against
the Persian king Darius.

Alexander the Great

100 BCE   50 BCE   0

88–64 BCE
The Mithridatic Wars: Rome
beats the kingdom of Pontus
and dominates Asia Minor

30 BCE
Rome annexes Egypt, the
last Hellenistic kingdom

VOLUME 2 *Chapters and contents*

THE BEGINNINGS OF CIVILIZATION IN EASTERN ASIA

THE CLASSICAL MEDITERRANEAN: GREECE

SERIES CONTENTS

INDEX

Page references to main text in roman, to box text in **bold** and to captions in *italic*.

ACKNOWLEDGMENTS

PICTURE CREDITS

The publishers wish to thank the following
for their kind permission to reproduce the
illustrations in this book:

Key

b bottom; c centre; t top; l left; r right
AAA: Ancient Art and Architecture Collection Ltd
AGE: A.G.E. Fotostock
AISA: Archivo Iconografico SA
AKG: AKG London
BAL: Bridgeman Art Library
BM: British Museum, London
BN: Bibliothèque Nationale, Paris
ET: e.t. Archive
MAN: Museo Arqueológico Nacional, Madrid
MANN: Museo Archeologico Nazionale, Naples
NAM: National Archaeological Museum, Athens
NMI: National Museum of India, New Dehli
RHPL: Robert Harding Picture Library
RMN: Réunion des Musées Nationaux, Paris
SAG: Staatliche Antikensammlungen und
    Glypothek, Munich
SK: Studio Kopperman
V&A: By courtesy of the board of trustees of the
    Victoria and Albert Museum, London
WFA: Werner Forman Archive

Front cover AKG / Erich Lessing / SAG
3 BAL / Oriental Museum, Durham University
7 AGE
9 RHPL
10 Godo-foto
11 AAA / Bruce Norman
12t RHPL / NMI
12b BAL / NMI
13tl AGE
13tr AGE
14t RHPL / NMI
14b RHPL / NMI
15 RHPL / Sassoon
16t AAA / R. Sheridan
16b AAA / R. Sheridan
17 AAA / R. Sheridan
18 Angelo Hornak / NMI
19 Michael Holford / Sarnath Museum, Varanasi
20 AAA
21 BAL / NMI
22 Michael Holford / BM
23 BAL / NMI
24t V&A
24b AAA / R. Sheridan
25 V&A
26 AGE / Alain Evrard
27 AGE / Alain Evrard
28 Panos Pictures / Cliff Venner
29 RHPL
30 AGE
32 China Photo Library
34t WFA / Yang-tzusshan, Szechwan
34b RHPL
35 ET
36 By courtesy of the Cultural Relics Bureau and
    the Metropolitan Museum of Art, New York
37l AISA
37r AAA / R. Sheridan

38 BN
39 BN
40 BM
41 *The Times*, London / Ray Main
42–3 RHPL
44 BAL / BM
46 AISA
47tc AISA
47tr AAA / R. Sheridan
48 AAA / R. Sheridan
49 AISA
51 BAL / Oriental Museum, Durham University
52l Zardoya / Magnum / Erich Lessing
52r BAL / BM
53 Michael Holford / Staatliches Museum für
    Völkerkunde, Munich
55 By courtesy of the Cultural Relics Bureau
    and the Metropolitan Museum of Art,
    New York
56 Godo-foto
57 AGE
59 AGE
60–61 Zardoya / Magnum / Erich Lessing
62t AISA
62b Godo-foto / Natural History Museum,
    New York
63t AISA
63b AISA / Archaeological Museum, Lima
64 ET / BM
65 AISA
68–9 Zardoya / Magnum / Erich Lessing
70 AKG / Erich Lessing
71 RHPL
73 Zardoya / Magnum / Erich Lessing
74 Jurgen Liepe
75 Erwin Böhm
76 AISA
77 AGE
78 Zardoya / Magnum / Erich Lessing
79 AISA
80 RHPL
83 AISA
84 BAL / Freud Museum, London
85 AGE
86 Scala / MANN
87t RHPL
87b AKG / Erich Lessing
88 Scala
89 ET
90t Kostas Kontos / NAM
90b RMN / Chuzeville / Louvre, Paris
91 Scala / Museo delle Terme, Rome
93 AGE
94t Scala / Museo Gregoriano Etrusco, Vatican
94b Scala / Museo delle Terme, Rome
95 Scala / Museo Pio Clementino, Vatican
96l AISA
96r AAA / R. Sheridan
97 AGE
98 BM
99t SK / SAG
99b Metropolitan Museum of Art, New York /
    Rogers Fund
100 SK / SAG
101t AAA / R. Sheridan
101b Scala / Museo Nazionale di Villa Giulia,
    Rome
102 Zardoya
103t MAN
103bl MAN
103br Jose Angel Gutiérrez
104 Scala / MANN
105 AAA / R. Sheridan

106 Scala / Museo Nazionale di Villa Giulia,
    Rome
107 Wadsworth Atheneum, Hartford,
    Conneticut / gift of J. Pierpont Morgan
108 AGE
109 AGE
110 AGE
112 BAL / Louvre, Paris
113 AISA / BN
114t AKG / Erich Lessing / Louvre, Paris
114b Sonia Halliday Photographs
115 AGE
117 AKG / Kunsthistorisches Museum, Vienna
118 AAA / R. Sheridan
119 AGE
120t SK / SAG
120b Scala / Il Duomo, Syracuse
122 Scala / MANN
123 Zardoya / Magnum / Erich Lessing
124t MAN
124b AAA / R. Sheridan
125t MAN
125b AKG / Antikensammlung, Berlin
126 BM
127t Scala / Acropolis Museum, Athens
127b RMN / Louvre, Paris
128 BM
130 Jose Angel Gutiérrez
131 BM
132 Scala / Agora Museum, Athens
133t Scala / Museo Pio Clementino, Vatican
134 Scala / Acropolis Museum, Athens
135 Kostas Kontos / NAM
136 Scala / Archaeological Museum, Olympia
137 AGE
138b AGE
139tl Jose Angel Gutiérrez
139tr Scala / Museo Pio Clementino, Vatican
140 Sonia Halliday Photographs
141 AISA / Musei Capitolini, Rome
142 AKG / Il Duomo di Anagni, Lazio
143 Scala / Museo Pio Clementino, Vatican
145t Scala / MANN
145b G. Dagli Orti / Louvre, Paris
146 Zardoya / Magnum / Erich Lessing
147 Firo-foto
148 MAN
149 AGE
150l AAA / R. Sheridan
150r BM
151 Zardoya / Magnum / Louvre, Paris
153 Scala
154 Kostas Kontos / NAM
155 AKG / Erich Lessing / Louvre, Paris
156 BAL / Archaeological Museum, Thessoloniki
157 Kostas Kontos / Archaeological Museum,
    Thessoloniki
158 Sonia Halliday Photographs
160 Scala / Acropolis Museum, Athens
162–3 Scala / MANN
164t Scala / Archaeological Museum, Istanbul
164c AAA / R. Sheridan
166l AGE
167 WFA / BM
168 AKG / Pergamon Museum, Berlin
169t Scala / MANN
169b AKG / Erich Lessing / Liebighaus,
    Frankfurt-am-Main
171 Zardoya / Magnum
172 AGE
173 Scala / Musei Capitolini, Rome
174 BAL / BN
175 AGE

176 AGE
177 Scala / Musei Capitolini, Rome
179 Scala / Museo Pio Clementino, Vatican

MAPS

Maps copyright © 1998 Debate pages 73, 87
Maps copyright © 1998 Helicon/Debate pages 8,
31, 58, 92, 121, 126, 161, 165, 178

TEXT CREDITS

The publishers wish to thank the following
for their kind permission to reproduce the
translations and copyright material in this book.
Every effort has been made to trace copyright
owners, but if anyone has been omitted we
apologize and will, if informed, make corrections
in any future edition.

p.25 extract from "The Chandogya Upanishad"
from The Upanishads, translated by Eknath
Easwaran (Arkana, 1988) copyright © The Blue
Mountain Center of Meditation, 1987. Repro-
duced by permission of Penguin Books Ltd.;
p.26 extract from "Vigilance" from *The
Dammapadha: the Sayings of the Buddha* by
Thomas Cleary. Copyright © 1994 by Thomas
Cleary. Reproduced by permission of Bantam
Books, a division of Random House, Inc.; pp.86
and 114, extracts from *The Histories* by
Herodotus, translated by Aubrey de Sélincourt,
revised by John Marincola (Penguin Classics
1954, Second revised edition 1996). Translation
copyright © 1954 by Aubrey de Sélincourt.
Revised edition copyright © John Maricola,
1996. Reproduced by permission of Penguin
Books Ltd.; p.126, extract from "Trojan
Women" from *Electra and Other Plays* by
Euripides, translated by John Davie, (Penguin
Classics, 1988) copyright © John Davie, 1988.
Reproduced by permission of Penguin Books
Ltd.; p.144 extract from *The Republic* by Plato,
translated by Desmond Lee (Penguin Classics
1955, Third revised edition 1987) copyright ©
Penguin Classics H. D. P. Lee, 1953, 1974, 1987.
Reproduced by permission of Penguin Books Ltd.